Singing Grammar

Teaching grammar through songs

MARK HANCOCK

CAMBRIDGE
UNIVERSITY PRESS

PUBLISHED BY THE PRESS SYNDICATE OF THE UNIVERSITY OF CAMBRIDGE
The Pitt Building, Trumpington Street, Cambridge, United Kingdom

CAMBRIDGE UNIVERSITY PRESS
The Edinburgh Building, Cambridge CB2 2RU, UK
40 West 20th Street, New York, NY 10011-4211, USA
477 Williamstown Road, Port Melbourne, VIC 3207, Australia
Ruiz de Alarcón 13, 28014 Madrid, Spain
Dock House, The Waterfront, Cape Town 8001, South Africa

http://www.cambridge.org

© Cambridge University Press 1998

This book is in copyright, which normally means that no reproduction of any part may take place without the written permission of Cambridge University Press. The copying of certain parts of it by individual teachers for use within their classrooms, however, is permitted without such formality. To aid identification, pages which are copiable by the teacher without further permission are identified by a separate copyright notice: From **Singing Grammar** by Mark Hancock © Cambridge University Press 1998   `PHOTOCOPIABLE`

First published 1998
Third printing 2002

Printed in the United Kingdom at the University Press, Cambridge

A catalogue record for this book is available from the British Library

ISBN 0 521 625424 Resource book
ISBN 0 521 625416 Cassette set

Contents

Contents map

6 **Acknowledgements**

7 **Introduction**
What is **Singing Grammar?**
Who is it for?
Why use songs?
Which songs?
How to make a song into a learning task
What is in the recordings
Managing songs and games in class: a troubleshooting guide
How to talk about pop music: a pop glossary

12 **How to use this book**
How the book is organized
How the units are organized

Section 1: Elementary

14 **1** Johnny's playing football
18 **2** Who, where, when?
22 **3** Getting up
26 **4** I can't hear you
30 **5** I've got exams
34 **6** What a crazy day!

Section 2: Pre-intermediate

38 **7** Space invader
42 **8** Dream of a pizza
46 **9** Blue train
50 **10** Happier than the birds
54 **11** I'd like to
58 **12** I was walking

Section 3: Intermediate

62 **13** If you're lonely
66 **14** Dangerous romance
70 **15** Josephine
74 **16** Sweet things
78 **17** In trouble again
82 **18** I've been waiting

Songbook

86 Finger positions
88 Lyrics and chords

Contents map

	Page	Grammar
Section 1: Elementary — age 10–13		
1 Johnny's playing football	14	present continuous
2 Who, where, when?	18	present simple (statement, *Wh-* question)
3 Getting up	22	affection verbs (*like, hate*, etc) followed by verb + *-ing*
4 I can't hear you	26	*can* (ability/request)
5 I've got exams	30	*have got*
6 What a crazy day!	34	irregular past tense verbs
Section 2: Pre-intermediate — age 13–15		
7 Space invader	38	present simple (1st, 3rd person affirmative, negative)
8 Dream of a pizza	42	countable and uncountable nouns, quantifiers
9 Blue train	46	adjective order
10 Happier than the birds	50	comparatives
11 I'd like to	54	*would like to do/like doing*
12 I was walking	58	past continuous/past simple
Section 3: Intermediate — age 15–18		
13 If you're lonely	62	first conditional
14 Dangerous romance	66	past simple narrative
15 Josephine	70	present perfect for experiences
16 Sweet things	74	*used to* for past habits and states
17 In trouble again	78	past perfect
18 I've been waiting	82	present perfect simple/continuous

Music and Song topic	Pronunciation and Vocabulary	Game
chant + slow version telling tales	contractions ('s, 're); classroom misbehaviour	whole class mime guessing game
chant + slow version a conversation about friends	silent *h* and *w* in *Wh-* questions, weak forms; *Wh-* question words	whole class bingo
chant + karaoke talking about likes and dislikes	sentence stress; chores and leisure activities	small groups card game (snap)
funk + karaoke asking about ability and giving instructions	vowel sounds /ɑː/ and /æ/; parts of body, movement	small groups physical response game
reggae + karaoke envy of boy for an animal with an easy life	word linking (final /t/ initial vowel sound)	small groups card game (happy families)
pop + karaoke narrating a strange day	sound and spelling of /e/; irregular verbs	pairs interviewing
rock + karaoke daily life of a computer game alien	word linking (final consonant initial vowel sound); daily routines, computers	small groups card guessing game
pop + karaoke a midnight snack	contractions (*aren't, isn't*), intrusive /r/; food, quantifiers	pairs board game
rock and roll + karaoke travelling home	word linking (consonant consonant); descriptive adjectives	small groups dominoes
rock ballad + karaoke comparing with a rival in love	weak forms (*as, than*); comparative adjectives	pairs order guessing game
calypso + karaoke inviting someone out	contraction (*I'd*), weak form (*to*); informal conversation (*well, oh, not too bad*, etc)	pairs battleships
pop + karaoke recalling a love at first sight	sound and spelling of /w/, weak forms (*was, were*); expressions of emotion	small groups deduction game
ballad + karaoke promising friendship	silent *r*, phonetic script; adjectives of feeling, metaphors	pairs card guessing game
jazz + karaoke the story of a gangster romance	past tense *-ed* endings; gangsters and police	individual/pairs maze
latin pop + karaoke building up courage to declare love	contractions (*I've, you've*); verbs or perception, cognition (*see, dream*, etc)	pairs board guessing game
ballad + karaoke betrayal of love and friendship	minimal pair /s/ and /z/; actions, habits and states	individual/pairs maze
rock + karaoke teenage misadventures	contractions (*I'd, we'd*), weak forms, phonetic script; reporting verbs of perception, cognition (*remember, notice*, etc)	small groups consequences
country + slow version being stood up on a date	linking (vowel vowel), intrusive sounds; phrasal verbs with *up*	small groups board game (snakes and ladders)

Acknowledgements

I would like to thank Nóirín Burke at Cambridge University Press for her support and wisdom throughout this project. I am also very grateful for the painstaking scrutiny and constructive suggestions provided by Tony Garside.

Cassette

Thanks to Liam Murphy for his enthusiasm and participation in early recordings of the material. I would also like to thank the following team in Madrid for their work in creating the pilot version of the tape:
Ramon Leál (production); Kike Fernandez Diaz (production, keyboards), Francis Garcia Diaz (arrangement, saxophone), Mike McDonald and Natalia Farrán Graves (lead vocals), Pilar Machi, Cristina Gonzalez and Susanna Peris (backing vocals), Jose Luis Ordoñez (electric guitar).

I am very grateful for the professionalism and artistry of the team in Brighton who colloborated to make the final version of the cassette:

Produced by:	Tim Douglass
Arranged and performed by:	Michael Bowes (drums and percussion)
	Gary Williams (bass guitar)
	Nico Sabatini (guitars)
	Mark Edwards (keyboards)
	Tim Douglass (keyboards)
	Graham Snell (saxophone)
Lead vocals:	Terry McMaster (songs 2, 5, 7, 9, 10, 12, 15, 17, 18)
	Victoria T Ford (songs 4, 8, 13, 14)
	Natalia Farrán Graves (songs 3, 6, 16)
	Jacqueline Austin (song 11)
	Russ Martin (songs 1, 2)
	George McMaster (song 2)
Chorus:	The Boys Choir of Varndean School, Brighton
	Sue Fairhurst, Susanna Miller
Backing vocals:	All the lead vocalists, and Gary Williams, Mark Hancock, Michael Bowes
Chant (opening, song 1)	Charlotte, Aaron, Daniel and the children of Albourne CEP School, Hassocks
Spoken instructions:	Michael Bowes
Engineer:	Trevor Bone

Thanks again to Tony Garside for his practical advice during the recording.

Book

The author would like to thank the following teachers, students and institutions for reviewing and trialling the material from *Singing Grammar* so thoroughly and for the practical suggestions for improvements:
Fernando Casales, Habana, Cuba; Laura Kazan, The English Centre, Istanbul, Turkey; Andrew Littlejohn, Pisa, Italy; Emma Murray, International House, Opole, Poland; Bob Obee, Athens, Greece; Nigel Pike, Cambridge, UK; Nicholas Shaw, Cambridge English Studies, La Coruña, Spain; Mike Rogers, English One, Seville, Spain; Aurea Mitiko Shinto, São Paulo, Brazil; Andy Taylor, Shane Language School, Bangkok, Thailand; Mark Thompson, King's College of English, Bangkok, Thailand.

The author and publishers are grateful to the following photographic sources and copyright holders for permission to reproduce material in *Singing Grammar*:
p.19 Pictor International for Hong Kong skyline and Getty Images/Will & Deni McIntyre for Sugarloaf moutain; p.28 Getty Images/Marc Schechter for Waikiki beach, Getty Images/Manfred Mehlig for Selva di Cadore, Italy and Getty Images/Anthony Cassidy for Amsterdam; p.37 John Walmsley for Market research; p.47 Pictor International for Locomotive and Mark Hancock for Plane; p.64 Pictor International for Man with virtual reality helmet.

Cover illustration Gecko Limited, Bicester, Oxon

Book illustrations Gecko Limited, Mark Hancock, Phil Healey, John Plumb, Sam Thompson

Page design Amanda Hancock

Book production Gecko Limited, Bicester, Oxon

Introduction

What is Singing Grammar?
Singing Grammar is a teacher's resource book containing photocopiable supplementary materials for use in the class. It is accompanied by two cassettes of songs. It is designed to provide a motivating alternative focus on various points of English grammar.

Who is it for?
Singing Grammar is for teachers of general English who are looking for ways to provide variety in their classes. The material is written principally with 10–18-year-old students in mind. The book is divided into three sections, the first for elementary students, the second for pre-intermediate and the third for intermediate. The Contents map indicates which parts of the age range each section is recommended for. However, it should be pointed out that the elementary section could provide useful revision for higher level students; similarly, teachers will find that songs suggested for younger students also appeal to older ones, and many adult classes will be receptive to the songs, too.

At the end of the book, there is a Songbook with lyrics and chords to enable teachers and students to play the songs on guitar or keyboard.

Why use songs?
Music motivates. People listen to music for pleasure. Teachers have for a long time recognized that they can use songs to motivate students and provide variety in a lesson. Variety is especially important for younger students, who often have very little internal motivation for entering a language classroom. There is widespread interest in pop songs among people of this age group, and such songs can be very profitably exploited in language-learning activities. The focus of this book is studying *grammar* through songs, but there are many other possibilities too. I will discuss these possibilities under three headings: *Listening*, *Language* and *Topic*.

Listening
Songs can provide practice in listening skills. Warm-up work can provide a basis for students to make *predictions* before listening. Listening activities can encourage *listening for gist* or *listening for detail*. Speaking, reading and writing skills may be involved in follow-up activities like those discussed under the heading *Topic* below.

Language
Songs can be used to focus on the form of the language, including grammar, vocabulary and pronunciation. Firstly, the song can be used *as a sample* of language to be analysed. This could involve activities such as the students answering concept questions about grammar features in the song, searching the song for antonyms or identifying certain pronunciation patterns. Secondly, the song can be used *as an exercise*. Students can be asked to do gap-fills, transformations, pronunciation drills, and so on using the lyric. In either case, the student can make use of the *mnemonic* quality of songs: the way words are much more memorable in combination with rhythm and melody. Students can call given language forms to memory simply by singing the song mentally, and this is something people even do involuntarily. The songs in this book are written to be especially suitable for grammar work, but there are also suggestions for vocabulary and pronunciation work.

Topic
Songs can provide topics for discussion and extension activities. *Characters* in the song can be used as a basis for role play, letter writing, and so on. The *plot* of the song can be a basis for story telling and imaginative reconstruction. *Poetry* in the song can be interpreted and converted into prose. The *musical style* of the song and its cultural background can be discussed.

Which songs?
Probably any song could be used for at least one of the activity types outlined above. The question is how to maximize the opportunities that the song offers. If you have a song you would like to use, you can select a suitable activity type by asking questions such as these:

1 *Would my class not dislike this song?*
  (The phrasing of this question is important: just because a student might not choose to listen to a certain song outside the classroom, it does not mean that the student would not enjoy it as part of a learning activity.)
2 *Are the lyrics of the song clearly audible?*
3 *Is the level of difficulty appropriate for my class?*
(If the answers to 2 and 3 are *yes*, then the song would probably be good for a listening skills activity.)
4 *Does the song provide a good illustration of a structure I want to present?*
5 *Does the song include a lexical field which fits well in the course?*
6 *Is the pronunciation natural enough to present a model?*
(If the answers to 4, 5 or 6 are *yes*, then the song may be good for a language-form activity.)
7 *Are there clear characters or an obvious plot in the lyric?*
8 *Could you discuss the poetic images or the cultural background of the song?*
(If the answers to 7 or 8 are *yes*, then the song would be good for a theme-based activity.)

Of course, it is easier to work from song to activity than the other way round. For instance, if you are looking for a song to illustrate a given structure, it can be very difficult. Even if you know the perfect song, you still have to find a cassette and the lyrics for it. **Singing Grammar** is written with this problem in mind. The Contents map enables the teacher to work from course requirements to song, and the recordings and lyrics are provided. The songs have been written attempting to elicit as many *yes* answers as possible to the above questions, making it possible to use a variety of activity types with each song.

Introduction

How to make a song into a learning task

The activities suggested here are classified according to their focus on skill, form or theme. More specific suggestions for using the songs in **Singing Grammar** are provided in the Teacher's notes of the units.

A Listening

A1 Prediction

Picture discussion: Find pictures to illustrate the song. Ask students to describe the pictures and predict what the song is about from them.

Key word discussion: Present some key words and/or the title from the lyrics and ask students to predict what the song is about.

Snippets: Play the first few seconds of the song and ask students to predict from the mood of the music what the song is about. This can be repeated, playing snippets and predicting right through the song.

Prediction: Ask students to do one of the activities from A3 below such as gap-filling or sequencing <u>before</u> listening, then listen to check.

A2 Listening for gist

Picture selection: Show students two or more alternative pictures, magazine photos perhaps, and ask them to say which one best matches the content/mood of the lyric and why.

Note-taking: Ask students to listen to the song and take notes — of key words, main characters or main events, for example.

Discourse-type recognition: Ask students to listen and identify the kind of discourse in the song: is it a dialogue? a narrative? a monologue in somebody's mind? Is it addressed to the listener? self-addressed?

Function recognition: Is the singer promising? warning? daydreaming? tale-telling? complaining? reminiscing? inviting? requesting?

A3 Listening for detail

Word-spotting: Present some key words from the lyric plus some not in the lyric. Ask students to circle the words they hear, and perhaps order the words which are in the song.

Gap-filling: Give students a copy of the lyric with some words erased. Ask them to listen and fill in the missing words. This can be made easier if you provide a jumbled list of the words erased.

Error-finding: Give students a copy of the lyric with some errors, for example wrong words, extra words or words missing. Ask them to listen and identify the errors.

Sequencing: Give students a copy of the lyric with the lines in the wrong order or cut into strips. Ask them to listen and put them in the right order.

Picture-sequencing: Give students pictures with scenes from the lyric. Ask them to listen and put the pictures in the correct order. They could suggest an order and a story before listening.

Picture differences: Give students pictures representing the lyric, but with some differences. Ask them to listen and indicate the inaccuracies in the picture.

Dictation: Play the song several times and ask students to write the words from the song or a section of it. Students could do this in teams and cooperate to complete the text.

Questions: Prepare comprehension questions. Ask students to listen and answer the questions.

True or false: Prepare true or false statements about the lyric and ask students to listen and decide if they are true or false.

B Language

The song may be used as a sample for analysis. Give the students copies of the lyric so they can work together to analyse linguistic features in the text. More specific suggestions will be given in each unit of this book. Alternatively, with a little more preparation, the teacher can turn the lyric into an exercise in one of the ways suggested below.

B1 Grammar

Tense-selecting: Erase the verbs and put the infinitive by the gap. Ask students to put the verbs in an appropriate tense. Listen to check.

Error-identifying: Give students a copy of the lyric containing grammatical errors and ask them to correct the errors. Listen to check.

Transformation: Ask students to transform the song entirely: from active to passive; from direct to reported speech; from masculine to feminine; from first person to third person; from affirmative to negative; from present to past. They could attempt to sing their transformed versions. Alternatively, you could transform the lyric yourself and ask the students to transform it back to the original and listen to check.

Word-ordering: Give lines from the song with words in a jumbled order. Ask them to order the words and listen to check.

B2 Vocabulary

Text reconstruction: Erase all the words in the lyric or parts of it, and number each gap. Ask students to listen once, then try to reconstruct the text by saying the number and the word they think goes in that gap. Make it easier by giving first letters or specifying the part of speech of the word.

Lexical transformation: Give students a copy of the text, but with words replaced by an antonym where possible. Ask students to convert the text to opposites and listen to check. Alternatively, you could ask students to prepare a transformed version of the song and perhaps sing it. They could replace words with synonyms.

Search: Ask students to search the text for lexically-related words, synonyms, antonyms, hyponyms or meronyms.

Lexical gaps: Give students a copy of the lyric with gaps. Make sure that it is possible to fill the gaps by looking at the context. Ask them to fill the gaps by guessing, then listen to check.

B3 Pronunciation

Sound search: Ask students to search the text for examples of a given sound, or for rhyming words.

Stress search: Ask students to search the text for words with a given stress pattern.

Script transformation: Give students a copy of the lyric with some or all of the words given in phonetic script. Ask them to convert these and listen to check.

Introduction

Drilling: Ask students to practise pronunciation by repeating certain parts of the lyric. Focus on a particular feature: weak forms; contractions; stress time; liaison. Specific suggestions are given in each unit of this book.

Singing: Ask students to sing along to the song, or chant the words to the music.

C Topic

C1 Characters

Diary-writing: Ask students to write diary entries for the characters.

Letters: Ask students to write letters to or from the characters, giving advice for example.

Role play: Ask students to role-play characters from the song.

Imagining: Ask students to extend the characters, imagining what they look like, do in their free time, would do in given situations, and so on.

C2 Plot

Summarizing: Ask students to summarize the events in the lyric.

Continuing: Ask students to continue the story. The continuation could be written as lyrics and sung.

Prior events: Ask students to imagine how the characters ended up in the situation they are in.

Reporting: Ask students to rewrite the lyric as a newspaper article.

Story-telling: Ask students to tell the story as a personal anecdote to a classmate. The classmate should respond with appropriate emotion, such as interest or sympathy.

C3 Lyric poetry

Genre transformation: Ask students to rewrite the lyric in a different genre or register: a dialogue; a speech; very formally; very informally; a TV report; a newspaper report; a passage from a novel.

Ambiguity: Discuss alternative interpretations of ambiguous passages from the lyric.

C4 Musical styles

Classification: Ask students to classify the musical style: chant; pop; rock and roll; folk; jazz; punk; rap; funk.

Culture reflection: Discuss how culture is reflected in the song; could this happen in your country? in any country? Could the male/female roles in this song be reversed? How old do you think this character must be?

Managing songs and games in class: a troubleshooting guide

Songs

When I started the tape, they just giggled.

The giggling probably started with one or two students who felt self-conscious about the music. Perhaps they like another kind of music and they do not want their classmates to think they identify with this kind. One way to get around this problem is not to present the song as something they are supposed to like. For instance, you could go straight to the detailed listening activity, such as sequencing. That way, the students are too busy with the task to be concerned about what the others think about them. Once students get more used to hearing songs in class, the giggling problem will probably reduce.

They won't sing.

The students may feel that they cannot sing, or that singing gives the wrong impression of themselves to the others in the class. You cannot force students to sing, but you can encourage them. For instance, you could drill the lines of the song as ordinary speech, without melody. They will probably accept this as a non-threatening classroom activity which they have done many times before. From there, it is a short step to putting a little rhythm into the words, and another short step to giving them a melody. Students who will not sing along to the song may be prepared to chant or speak with it. Those students who will not even do that are at least getting some listening practice, and the song may 'stick in their heads' anyway.

They think songs are a waste of time.

Many students, particularly older ones, feel that they only learn from serious-looking activities. You could explain the linguistic aims of the song-based activity before you begin, perhaps using the categories of *Listening*, *Language* and *Topic* outlined above. After the activity, summarize or ask students to summarize what language points they covered in the task. They could put this summary in their notebooks.

They go crazy if I play a song.

Younger students in particular may start dancing and banging desks. You could divide the class into teams and get them to complete the activity competitively. Then play the song at such a low volume that they must be really attentive to hear it. Later on, when it comes to asking them to sing along, perhaps their noisy reaction is not really a problem after all. But check this with your colleague in the next room!

There's never enough time left at the end to do a song.

Your song-based activity need not be left until the end. Songs are good for warming up the class too. And if the activity has a serious teaching point, why not make it the basis for the entire lesson?

Introduction

Games

> When they're in groups, they just mess around.

Most of the games in this book involve grouping the students. The easiest way to do this is to ask students to work with the person/people sitting nearest to them. However, you may notice that the group becomes too familiar with one another and do not take the task seriously. In this case, students may benefit from working in other groupings. You might decide to organize this yourself, for example by putting students with stronger and weaker levels of English together. Alternatively, you could use a more random method. For example, you could ask the class to put themselves in line according to alphabetical order of their names or order of birthdays and then form a group with their neighbours in the line.

> They never seem to understand the rules.

Most games will work better if you demonstrate them as well as explain the rules. To do this, you could play the game yourself with volunteers from the class. You may want to make large or overhead transparency versions of a few cards, the game board or the puzzle to help with the demonstration.

> They did most of the game in their own language.

In monolingual classes, students typically use their native language to organize the game: to discuss whose turn it is, to say when someone has broken a rule, to say when the game has finished, and so on. They also tend to ask for translations in their native language. In this way, they miss useful practice opportunities.

A good way to raise their awareness of this is to record one or more groups during the activity. Play the tape back to the class and ask them to identify and translate native language expressions into English. Note that students often whisper when they use their native language in group work, so it may only be the speaker who can make out what they said. They could list these expressions in their notebooks. They can then refer to the list and add to it in future games.

> They got into a fight about who should start.

Usually, students can decide who starts peacefully. However, sometimes the one with the strongest personality always gets to choose, or they spend valuable time arguing. You could suggest more random methods. For example, they could play in reverse alphabetical order of names, or in order of who lives nearest to the school, or in order of who can write the most names of animals in one minute.

> They might make mistakes when they're in groups.

Group work gives students a valuable opportunity to practise language in a different social setting. Students who are shy to speak in front of the whole class may find it easier in a pair or small group. And of course, in groups they get a much greater percentage of talking time per person. However, students may make mistakes or get into difficulties in group work. You could move around the class monitoring language and checking that the game is proceeding smoothly. In some cases, for example when a group is playing wrongly, you may want to intervene. In other cases, for example when a student makes a grammar mistake, you could leave the group to finish the game and review that point with the student or with the class at the end. Your moving around the class also gives students the chance to ask questions if they are having a problem.

> They never finish at the same time.

If a group finishes early, ask them if they would like to play again. If they have had enough, you could provide a filler activity such as a puzzle. Alternatively, you could invite them to be responsible for monitoring other groups. If a group is still playing when the others have finished, you could ask them to calculate their score so far, and find the winner in that way.

What is in the recordings

The cassettes contain the songs for the eighteen units. There are a variety of musical styles. Many of the songs have an *echo* format. This is where the lead singer sings a line and then the backing vocals repeat it. When the students sing, they can then sing along with this. Other songs have a *question and answer* format, where there are two different singers or groups of singers and they sing a dialogue. With these, you could divide the class into two groups and ask each group to take one part in the dialogue.

Most songs have a *karaoke version*. This is the music of the song without the voice of the singer or one of the singers. This allows the students to provide the vocals themselves or sing verses that they have written themselves. On the karaoke versions, there are beats with a drum stick to tell the students when to start singing.

For some of the songs, a *slow version* is included. This is to allow the students to get used to the pronunciation at a slower speed before they sing the final version of the song.

If your class enjoys singing, you could have singing sessions where you recycle songs they have already done. You could tape the class singing and perhaps give students a copy of this tape at the end of the course.

Introduction

How to talk about pop music: a pop glossary

You could present special vocabulary to enable students to discuss music. Here is a short glossary, arranged according to which aspect of music students want to talk about, which you may want to photocopy for them.

Talking about a song

beat main rhythm of a song

chorus part of a song which is repeated after each verse

intro (introduction) part of a song before the singer begins

lyric words of a song

riff short repeated tune by one instrument such as the guitar

solo part of a song where one person plays alone or with the others in the background

tune series of musical notes; the music, not the words

Talking about a band

backing vocals singers who support the lead singer

bassist person who plays bass guitar

brass section part of a group playing brass instruments like saxophone and trumpet

drummer person who plays drums

group/band a number of musicians who perform together

lead guitarist guitar player who plays the riffs and solos in a band

keyboard player person who plays piano, synthesizer or keyboards

lead singer person who sings the complete lyric of the song

rhythm section part of a band including drummer, bassist and guitarist

Talking about a concert

amps (amplifiers) machines to increase the volume of the instruments

applause clapping and shouting from the audience

encore extra songs after the applause at the end of a gig

gig pop concert

mike (microphone) machine singers hold to increase the volume of their voice

opening number first song of a gig

speakers large boxes where the sound comes out

venue place where the gig happens

Talking about recorded music

album complete record, tape or CD, usually with around 15 songs

cover version version of a song which was written and made famous by another band

hit track which becomes really popular and is played a lot on the radio

instrumental track with no singer or lyric

single track which is released separately on a small record, tape or CD, often used in discos by the disc jockey

track one song from an album

How to use this book

How the book is organized

Level
This book is divided into three sections. The first section is suitable for elementary students, the second for pre-intermediate and the third for intermediate. In many cases, the song could be adapted for a different level. This would involve the teacher making their own activity or songsheet, perhaps using one of the ideas from the Introduction above.

Age
The three sections are also organized by age. The book is designed primarily for an age range of ten to eighteen years old. The first section is more suitable for the bottom end of this range (about ten to thirteen), the second section for the middle (about thirteen to fifteen) and the last section for the top end (about fifteen to eighteen). However, this is only a guide, and many songs have a wider suitability and could also be used with adults.

Access
The book is designed as a source of supplementary materials. Many classes will be using a coursebook or following a syllabus, and the Contents map of this book is designed to allow the teacher to select a song which reinforces a language point in this coursebook or syllabus. The main point of access is the grammar indicated for the unit, but teachers may also select a song for its pronunciation focus, vocabulary or topic area.

Timing
Each unit of this book should take about one hour in the classroom if the teacher uses all three of the photocopiable pages. However, a unit could easily take longer if the teacher uses the extension suggestions and the students respond well to these. If the teacher decides to use only the *Songsheet*, it will take much less time, between ten and twenty minutes.

How the units are organized

There are eighteen units in the book, three in each section. Each unit consists of four pages: *Teacher's notes*, *Songsheet*, *Grammar page* and *Game page*. The contents of these pages plus general tips on how to use them are given opposite.

How to use this book

Teacher's notes

* **Title**

* **Summary of contents**

* **Complete song lyrics**

* **Songsheet** notes
Notes on listening, pronunciation and singing activities. In many cases, these also suggest vocabulary and topic extension activities.

* **Grammar page** notes
Tips on exploiting and extending the exercises.

* **Game page** notes
Notes on preparing and setting up the game activities.

Songsheet (photocopiable)

* **Pre-listening (usually pictures)**
If you have an overhead projector, you could copy the pictures onto a transparency and project it. This helps to focus attention and prevents students seeing the listening activity while doing the pre-listening activity. Alternatively, ask students to fold their copy of the Songsheet in half so they can only see the pictures. There is a dotted line to show students where to fold.

Most units begin with a prediction activity and a first listening before students see the lyric. With these activities, it is best to check answers as a class but not correct. Students will be able to correct for themselves when they see the lyric.

* **Listening activities**
Where the listening activity is sequencing, you may want to cut the lines into strips for the students to put in order. If you can photocopy onto card, these strips will be re-usable in future lessons. When students have sequenced the lines of the song, you could ask them to copy the lyric to sing from and to keep as a permanent copy.

Most Songsheets may be done by students working on their own or as pair work. However, in some cases, the Songsheet must be cut into parts A and B to form an information-gap pair work activity. If you have an odd number of students in your class, you could have two students with part A working with one student with part B.

Grammar page (photocopiable)

* **Grammar exercises**
These include exercises to present and/or practise the grammar point of the unit. In many cases, the last exercise provides a model of the language needed for the Game page activity.

Most Grammar page exercises involve students writing their answers on their own, though many are suitable for pair work, too. If your students are working at about the same speed, you could check the answers as a class exercise by exercise. However, to provide more flexibility, the answer key is provided at the bottom of the page. With this, you can ask students to self-correct. If you donot wish your students to see this, you can cut the key off and give it to them as a slip of paper at the end, or position the book on the photocopier in such a way that the key is left off the copy.

Game page (photocopiable)

* **Game: board, puzzle, cards, etc**
For many of the games, you will need to cut out cards. If you photocopy these onto card, they will be re-usable in future lessons. Alternatively, you could provide scissors and ask students to cut out the cards.

* **Rules (in many of the units)**
For group work games, rules are provided so that groups can check they are playing correctly during the game.

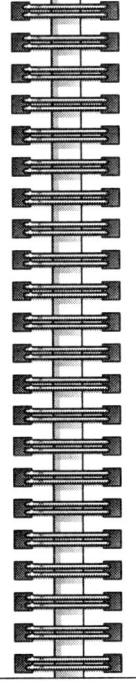

13

SECTION ONE ELEMENTARY

Grammar
present continuous

Music
chant + slow version

Topic
The topic in this song is children 'telling tales' on each other. For example, in the first verse, perhaps another child shouts out that Johnny is playing football in his school clothes in order to get Johnny into trouble. Listen to line 1 of the song. This melody, known as the 'cat call', is frequently used by children to tease each other, both in the UK and other parts of the world. Listen to line 5. This melody is often used in the UK and other places when someone is being called.
This song is an echo-chant: each time the lead singer sings a line, the backing vocals repeat that line.

Johnny's playing football
Johnny's playing football
He's wearing all his school clothes
  and getting very dirty
Johnny! Your mother's coming!
Johnny! Your mother's coming!

Mary's eating chocolate
Mary's eating chocolate
She's eating lots of chocolate
  and now she isn't hungry
Mary! Your dinner's ready!
Mary! Your dinner's ready!

The kids are drawing pictures
The kids are drawing pictures
They aren't doing the exercise
  they're just drawing pictures
Kids! The teacher's looking!
Kids! The teacher's looking!

Johnny's playing football

Songsheet

1 Prediction: Ask students to fold the Songsheet so they can only see the pictures. Students describe the pictures and predict what the song is about. As a hint, point out the one tale-telling child in each picture. If necessary, prompt students with questions like *Is the boy wearing sports clothes?* and *What is the friend saying?*
2 Gist: Play the song. Students check their predictions.
3 Students unfold the Songsheet and separate the words. Play the song again. Students listen and check.
4 Students add the apostrophes. Point out that there are several examples of the contraction of *is*: *'s*.
5 Pronunciation: To help with the difficult third/fourth line in each verse, you could 'backchain', that is, model it for the class to repeat like this:
very dirty   and getting very dirty   school clothes and getting very dirty …
Note: In this song, the auxiliary *'s* is pronounced /z/. In some cases you could drill this by tying the auxiliary to the next word, for example *Mary zeating*. The auxiliary *'re* is pronounced as a schwa /ə/. You could drill it like this: *The kid /zə/ drawing*.
6 The class could sing along to the song. If they find this difficult to the full speed version, let them sing to the slow version first.
7 Extension: Students could write more verses of their own and try to sing them with the same melody as the song.

Grammar page

1 Students underline the present simple or present continuous in exercise A.
Note: *He is always telling tales* (present continuous to show disapproval/irritation) is a possible alternative answer to *He tells tales*.
2 Exercise B focuses on agreement between pronoun, auxiliary and verb form.
3 Exercise C provides more written practice of the structure. As an extension, students could write a similar poem of their own.

Game page

WHOLE CLASS ACTIVITY

Preparation: Copy the set of cards (one set for the whole class) and cut them out.
1 Ask a volunteer (or demonstrate this yourself) to come to the front of the class, read a card and then mime the action.
2 The rest of the class should report what the person is doing, eg *Olga's eating bubble gum!* They could use the same tale-telling intonation from the song, since all the actions are forms of classroom misbehaviour.
3 The person who is miming indicates whether guesses are correct by nodding or shaking their head. If the answer is nearly correct, they say this or make a gesture.
4 Continue by asking more volunteers to come and mime actions on the cards.

1 JOHNNY'S PLAYING FOOTBALL — Songsheet

A Look at the pictures and say what the song is about. Listen and check.

Johnny

Mary

The kids

B Draw lines between the words. Then listen to the song again.

Example: *Johnnys/playing*

JohnnysplayingfootballJohnnysplaying football
Heswearingallhisschoolclothesand gettingverydirty

Johnny! Your mother's coming!
Johnny! Your mother's coming!

MaryseatingchocolateMaryseating chocolate
Sheseatinglotsofchocolateandnowsheisnt hungry

Mary! Your dinner's ready!
Mary! Your dinner's ready!

ThekidsaredrawingpicturesThekidsare drawingpictures
Theyarentdoingtheexersisetheyrejust drawingpictures

Kids! The teacher's looking!
Kids! The teacher's looking!

C Add apostrophes (') to the song.

Example: *Johnny's playing*

From **Singing Grammar** by Mark Hancock © Cambridge University Press 1998

Grammar page JOHNNY'S PLAYING FOOTBALL **1**

A Read this letter and choose the best tense.

Dear Billy,
I'm bored. My friends are in trouble and they can't play this evening. Johnny <u>washes/is washing</u> clothes. He <u>likes/is liking</u> football, and sometimes he <u>gets/is getting</u> his school clothes dirty. Today, for example!

Mary <u>washes up/is washing up</u>. Her mother is angry with her about eating chocolate before dinner. Mary <u>hates/is hating</u> her little brother. He always <u>tells/is telling</u> tales on her. Poor Mary!

The kids are still at school. They <u>write/are writing</u> 'Good students <u>don't draw/aren't drawing</u> pictures in class.' 1,000 times.

I <u>watch/am watching</u> TV on my own. Why are my friends so naughty?!

Love from
Sarah

B Make six sentences from these words and phrases:

I'm   Do you   like basketball.   plays the guitar.   enjoying the film?   He

writing sentences.   I   raining.   understand?   It's   Are you

C Complete this poem with the words in brackets.

Good Students Don't ...
The sun is shining
The birds are singing

(the children/laugh) _____
(the babies/cry)   _____
(my friends/play)   _____
(the time/pass)   _____
(the teacher/watch) _____

And I'm sitting here writing:
'Good students don't
Look out of the window.'

From **Singing Grammar** by Mark Hancock © Cambridge University Press 1998 **PHOTOCOPIABLE**

answers

A is washing; likes; gets; is washing up; hates; tells; are writing; don't draw; am watching

B I'm writing sentences. Do you understand? Are you enjoying the film? He plays the guitar. I like basketball. It's raining.

C The children are laughing. The babies are crying. My friends are playing. The time is passing. The teacher is watching.

16

1 JOHNNY'S PLAYING FOOTBALL **Game page**

EATING BUBBLE GUM	READING A COMIC	COPYING SOMEONE'S WORK
LISTENING TO YOUR WALKMAN	MAKING A PAPER PLANE	WRITING ON THE DESK
EATING NUTS	DRAWING A PICTURE OF SOMEBODY	READING A MAGAZINE
SLEEPING	LOOKING OUT OF THE WINDOW	PLAYING A COMPUTER GAME
THROWING BALLS OF PAPER	PLAYING CARDS	TALKING TO A FRIEND
COPYING IN THE EXAM	GIVING A NOTE TO A FRIEND	DRINKING COLA

From **Singing Grammar** by Mark Hancock © Cambridge University Press 1998 *PHOTOCOPIABLE* 17

SECTION ONE ELEMENTARY

Grammar
present simple (statement, Wh- question)

Music
chant + slow version

Topic
This song has the form of a dialogue. One voice begins a conversation about friends. The other voice displays interest in the conversation by asking for more details. The story gradually emerges that there is a love triangle between the friends mentioned: *John* loves *Jill*, but *Jill* loves *Jim*.

Who, where, when? Who, where, when?

I've got a friend and his name's John
Where does he come from?
Hong Kong!

John goes to school at half past nine
When does he come home?
At five!

John plays football some weekends
Who does he play with?
With friends!

John's got a girlfriend, her name's Jill
Where does she come from?
Brazil!

Jill has a band with a group of friends
When do they practise?
Weekends!

Jill plays the trumpet and the trombone
Where does she practise?
At home!

John loves Jill but she doesn't love him
Who does she love, then?
... JIM!

Who, where, when?

Songsheet

1 Prediction: Ask students to fold the Songsheet so they can only see the pictures. Students look at the pictures and predict what the song is about.
2 Play the song. Students number the pictures (in the boxes provided) in the order they are mentioned. (Answers: 1E, 2C, 3I, 4B, 5A, 6H, 7G, 8F, 9D)
3 Detail: Prepare and ask comprehension questions about the song. Here are some possibilities: *What time does John go to school? What does John do at weekends? What's John's girlfriend's name? What instruments does Jill play?* Students answer without looking at the lyrics.
4 Students unfold the Songsheet and order the jumbled questions. Play the song again for them to check their answers.
5 Pronunciation (sounds): Ask which of the three question words in the title have a silent *h* (*where, when*) and which has a silent *w* (*who*).
6 Pronunciation (rhythm): Students repeat the song. Pause the song after each line. Ask them to keep the same rhythm as in the song. Focus on the weak forms in the questions: *does he; does she; do they*.
7 Divide the class into two groups. One group sings the statements in the song, the other group sings the questions. Then they could swap roles and sing it again. They could clap to the beat. If they have difficulty with the full speed version, let them sing to the slow version first.
8 Extension: Students in pairs could perform the lyric as a dialogue in a normal voice. Then they could try it again changing the names and the details of their 'friends'. Asking questions about what someone is telling you is a conversational strategy which encourages the other person to continue. In this activity, the students practise this strategy.

Grammar page

1 Remind students that some sentences in exercise A are <u>correct</u>; you could name number 1 as an example.
Note: In the present simple tense, it is necessary to add the auxiliary *do* or *does* in the question unless the verb is *be*. Also, if the question is not a *yes/no* question (that is, a question where the answer is *yes* or *no*), it is necessary to add a *Wh-* pronoun (*who, where, when, what, how, why, which*).
2 Before doing exercise B, you could ask students to cover the interview with their hand and look at the picture and text in the speech bubble. The text is very vague; you could ask them to speculate about the missing details and the vague words (*some, something, somewhere*). For example, ask *What time do you think he gets up? What does he have for breakfast?*
3 Students practise the interview in pairs, taking it in turns to play each role.

Game page

WHOLE CLASS ACTIVITY
Preparation: Copy the page and cut it into four cards. You will need one card for each student.
1 Give out the cards. There are four different versions; students should have a different one from the students they are sitting next to.
2 On the sheets, there are questions with a space for an answer. The objective is for the students to fill in these spaces. Explain that you will read out answers and students must write these answers in the spaces if they have the correct question.
3 When a student gets a line from left to right or top to bottom across their bingo card, they should call out *Bingo!* Glance over their card to ensure it is correct and give a small prize (eg their name in fancy letters on the blackboard).
4 Give a bigger prize (eg their name in larger letters) to the first student to complete their bingo card.
5 Read out the answers from this list:
  1 *Yes, I do* **2** *No, I'm not* **3** *Finland* **4** *His mother*
  5 *At one thirty* **6** *Go out with my friends* **7** *Because it's near*
  8 *Yes, he does* **9** *No, she isn't* **10** *Yes, they do* **11** *No, it isn't*
  12 *Yes, she does* **13** *No, he isn't* **14** *(Say your own name)*

2 WHO, WHERE, WHEN?

Songsheet

A Look at the pictures. What is this song about?

B Listen and number the pictures in the correct order.

C Put the words in the correct order to make the questions. Then listen and check.

Who, where, when? Who, where, when?

I've got a friend and his name's John
come does from he where

_____?
Hong Kong!

John goes to school at half past nine
does when home he come

_____?
At five!

John plays football some weekends
who he play with does

_____?
With friends!

John's got a girlfriend, her name's Jill
she from where come does

_____?
Brazil!

Jill has a band with a group of friends
practise do when they

_____?
Weekends!

Jill plays the trumpet and the trombone
she where practise does

_____?
At home!

John loves Jill but she doesn't love him
does she who love

_____, then?
... JIM!

From **Singing Grammar** by Mark Hancock © Cambridge University Press 1998 **PHOTOCOPIABLE**

Grammar page

WHO, WHERE, WHEN? **2**

A Some of these questions are incorrect. Tick (✓) the correct ones and add one of these words to the incorrect ones:

do   does   who   where   when   what

Example: Where / you come from?

1 Is your name Peter?
2 Are you tired?
3 Where you go to school?
4 You like music?
5 Is she with you?
6 He live here?
7 Is your name?
8 Do you live in England?
9 Do you live?
10 When she go to bed?
11 You speak English?
12 Is it cold outside?
13 You understand?
14 Are my glasses?
15 Are you asleep?
16 Do you live with?
17 When the train leave?
18 Do you do in the evenings?
19 Does the class finish?
20 Is this the end?

B This is what Pete Sweet says about his daily life. He doesn't give us many details, so you decide to interview him. Write your questions.

I get up very late and I have something great for breakfast. Then I go to work. I really like my job! I have something for lunch. Later, I go home. I do something before dinner. After dinner I go somewhere. I meet some people and we do something.

1 You : _____ ?
   Oh, about half past ten or eleven.

2 You : _____ ?
   A cake and two or three packets of biscuits.

3 You : _____ ?
   I'm a chocolate taster. I work at a chocolate factory.

4 You : _____ ?
   I usually have a sugar sandwich.

5 You : _____ ?
   About three o'clock.

6 You : _____ ?
   I sleep for an hour or two before dinner.

7 You : _____ ?
   The social club.

8 You : _____ ?
   My friends from the factory.

9 You : _____ ?
   We play cards and eat chocolate.

From **Singing Grammar** by Mark Hancock © Cambridge University Press 1998   **PHOTOCOPIABLE**

Answers

A 1 correct 2 correct 3 Where do you go to school? 4 Do you like music? 5 correct 6 Does he live here? 7 What is your name? 8 correct 9 Where do you live? 10 When does she go to bed? 11 Do you speak English? 12 correct 13 Do you understand? 14 Where are my glasses? 15 correct 16 Who do you live with? 17 When does the train leave? 18 What do you do in the evenings? 19 When does the class finish? 20 correct

B 1 What time do you get up? 2 What do you have for breakfast? 3 What do you do?/What's your job? 4 What do you have for lunch? 5 What time do you go home? 6 What do you do before dinner? 7 Where do you go after dinner? 8 Who do you meet there?/go with? 9 What do you do with them?

2 WHO, WHERE, WHEN? **Game page**

Who, where, when? 1

Is he married?	When do they have lunch?	Why do you walk to school?
Does he like music?	Where do you come from?	Do they live here?
What do you do at weekends?	What is your name?	Do you speak Spanish?

Who, where, when? 2

Why do you walk to school?	What is your name?	When do they have lunch?
Is she a student?	Who does he live with?	Is it sunny?
Does she play tennis?	Do you speak Spanish?	Are you French?

Who, where, when? 3

Do you speak Spanish?	Is he married?	Where do you come from?
Is it sunny?	When do they have lunch?	Does he like music?
Why do you walk to school?	Who does he live with?	What is your name?

Who, where, when? 4

Why do you walk to school?	Do they live here?	Are you French?
What is your name?	What do you do at weekends?	Is she a student?
Who does he live with?	When do they have lunch?	Does she play tennis?

From **Singing Grammar** by Mark Hancock © Cambridge University Press 1998 *PHOTOCOPIABLE*

SECTION ONE ELEMENTARY

Grammar
affection verbs (*like, hate*, etc) followed by verb + *-ing*

Music
chant + karaoke

Topic
This song has the form of a dialogue about likes and dislikes. The backing vocals ask questions and the lead singer answers. When the song is repeated, it is in the third person with *he*.

**Do you like getting up
And going to school?
No no! I enjoy having fun**

**Do you like sitting down
And doing exams?
No no! I enjoy watching films**

**Do you like washing up
And cleaning your room?
No no! I enjoy playing games**

**I don't like housework
And I hate homework
I love relaxing with my friends**

*

Does he like getting up ...

Getting up

Songsheet

Prediction: Ask students to fold the Songsheet so they can only see the pictures. Students predict words they will hear in the song. List their suggestions on the board.
2 Detail: Play the first half of the song, to where you see the asterisk (*) in the lyric. Students listen for the words on the board.
3 Students unfold the Songsheet and play this text completion game: they call out their suggestions one by one, eg *Number five — up*, and you tell them if that is correct or not. They need not guess in order, 1, 2, 3, etc; they can start in the middle if they prefer. For your purposes, it would be helpful to number the words on your copy of the lyric so you can respond quickly to their guesses. To do this game, students must use their knowledge of grammar and word order since there is too much to remember from the song. You can make this into a competitive game by dividing the class into two teams. Give a point for each correct guess. When all the gaps have been filled, play the song to the asterisk again.
4 Grammar: Students rewrite or recite the lyric in the third person, beginning *Does he like getting up ...* Then they listen to the second half of the song to check.
5 Vocabulary: Students classify the activities in the song under these categories: *leisure activities; housework; schoolwork*. Note the difference between *housework* and *homework*.
6 Pronunciation: Students sing along with the backing vocals in the song. You could ask them to pronounce the questions slowly first. Divide the song into sections and show the rhythm pattern for each section, eg *Do you like* (OoO) / *getting up* (OoO) / *and going to school* (oOooO). These rhythm patterns are the same for all three questions.
Note: The weak form of *and* is used, with the *d* not pronounced.
7 Split the class into two groups; one group sings with the lead singer in the song, the other group sings with the backing vocals. Once the students are confident, they could sing to the karaoke version.

Grammar page

1 Students could do exercise A in pairs and then role-play the dialogue.
2 Exercise B concerns the difference of degree from *love* to *hate*.
Note: After most of these verbs, an infinitive could be used with very little difference in meaning. However, an infinitive isn't used after *enjoy*, so the verb + *-ing* form is perhaps more useful at this stage.
3 Students could work in pairs again for exercise C. They could write a paragraph like the one in exercise A about the student they interviewed.
4 Exercise D is a memory game. You could set a time limit of two or three minutes for them to write their answers.
5 Extension: Students could prepare and perform interviews like the one in exercise A, but with unusual characters such as Count Dracula. For example: *Do you like drinking milk? — No, but I love drinking blood!*

Game page

SMALL GROUPS ACTIVITY
Preparation: Make one copy of the game page for every group of three or four students. Cut out the cards or provide scissors for your students to do this.
1 Put the students into groups of three or four and give each group the cards and rules sheet, which will be left over when the cards have been cut out.
2 Students draw five columns on a piece of paper with one of *love, like, OK, dislike, hate* at the top of each column. Then ask them to classify the activities in rule 3 into these columns, according to their own opinion. One student in each group could read the list aloud for the other members of the group.
3 Demonstrate the game with two volunteers. Ask them to come to the front with their paper with the five columns. Take the role of dealer: place cards on the table and give your opinion, eg *I like drawing pictures*. If the volunteers have the same opinion, they can win the card by putting their hand on it and saying *So do I!* If both volunteers share your opinion, the fastest to do this will win the card.
4 Point out the sentence structure for the opinion *OK* is different.
5 Leave the groups to play the game.

3 GETTING UP — Songsheet

A Look at the pictures. Predict some words in this song.

B Listen and check your predictions.

C Guess the missing words of the song. Use your memory and your knowledge of grammar!
Example: *Number 5 — up!*

___ ___ ___ ___ up ___ ___ ___ ___ ?
1   2   3   4   5   6   7   8   9

No no! I enjoy having fun

___ ___ ___ ___ ___ ___ ___ ___ ?
10   11   12   13   14   15   16   17

No no! I enjoy watching films

___ ___ ___ ___ ___ ___ ___ ___ ___ ?
18   19   20   21   22   23   24   25   26

No no! I enjoy playing games

I don't like housework
And I hate homework
I love relaxing with my friends

D Listen again to check your answers.

E The second part of the song is similar, but it begins *Does he like getting up ...*
Can you continue it? Listen and check.

From **Singing Grammar** by Mark Hancock © Cambridge University Press 1998

Grammar page

GETTING UP 3

A Read this Penfriend Profile and complete the interview.

> *Linda gets up early but she doesn't like it. She goes to school but she hates it. After school, she plays with her friends and she loves that. She thinks reading is OK. In the evening, she watches videos, and she enjoys that.*

Interviewer: Linda, do you like (1) _____ up early?

Linda: No, I don't.

Interviewer: And do you (2) _____ _____ to school?

Linda: No, I (3) _____ it.

Interviewer: Do you like (4) _____ with your friends?

Linda: Yes, I love playing with my friends.

Interviewer: Really? And do you like (5) _____?

Linda: Yes, it's OK.

Interviewer: And one more question, do you like (6) _____ videos?

Linda: Yes, I enjoy that.

B What does Linda like doing? Put these activities in order, from very good to very bad:

getting up early   reading   going to school
playing with friends   watching videos

C Think of five activities: one you love, one you like, one you think is OK, one you dislike and one you hate.

love = _____

like = _____

OK = _____

dislike = _____

hate = _____

Write these activities in a list in a different order. Don't say if you like the activity or not. Exchange lists with another student. Interview the other student as in exercise A.

D Look at this picture of Martin's room for one minute. Then turn the paper over and write about Martin's hobbies.
Example: *I think he likes playing tennis.*

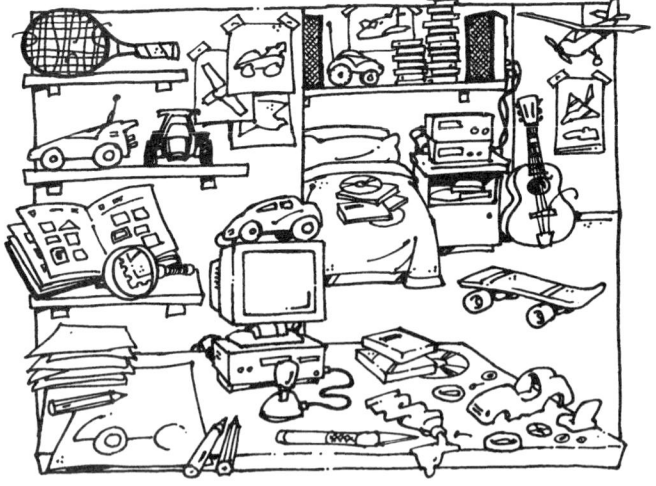

From **Singing Grammar** by Mark Hancock © Cambridge University Press 1998   **PHOTOCOPIABLE**

---

answers

A 1 getting 2 like going 3 hate 4 playing 5 reading 6 watching

B 1 playing with friends 2 watching videos 3 reading 4 getting up early 5 going to school

D He likes: listening to music; playing tennis; playing the guitar; playing computer games; drawing; skateboarding; collecting stamps; making models

3 GETTING UP

Game page

Rules

1 Play this game in groups of three or four.

2 On a piece of paper, draw five columns. At the top of each column, write these titles:
love   like   OK   dislike   hate

3 Write these activities under each title, in your opinion.
swimming cycling playing computer games
watching films listening to music watching TV
eating vegetables drinking coffee playing cards
drinking cola washing up doing homework
doing exams cleaning my room going to the
dentist cooking getting up reading
doing maths walking drawing pictures

4 In each game, one person is the dealer. The dealer keeps all the cards in her or his hand.

5 The dealer puts the cards on the table, one by one. At the same time, the dealer gives an opinion about the activity on the card.
Example: If the activity on the card is *swimming*, the dealer can say *I dislike swimming*.

The dealer uses one of these sentence forms:

I love _____

I like _____

I think _____ *is OK.*

I dislike _____

I hate _____

6 The aim of the game is for the players to win cards. You can win a card if you have the same opinion as the dealer. For example, you put *swimming* under the title *dislike* on your paper. If the dealer says *I dislike swimming*, you can put your hand on the card and say *So do I!* The first player to do this wins the card.

7 The player with most cards at the end wins.

8 Play the game again with a different dealer.

SWIMMING	CYCLING	PLAYING COMPUTER GAMES
WATCHING FILMS	LISTENING TO MUSIC	WATCHING TV
EATING VEGETABLES	DRINKING COFFEE	PLAYING CARDS
DRINKING COLA	WASHING UP	DOING HOMEWORK
DOING EXAMS	CLEANING MY ROOM	GOING TO THE DENTIST
COOKING	GETTING UP	READING
DOING MATHS	WALKING	DRAWING PICTURES

From **Singing Grammar** by Mark Hancock © Cambridge University Press 1998 **PHOTOCOPIABLE**

SECTION ONE ELEMENTARY
4

Grammar
can (ability/request)

Music
funk + karaoke

Topic
This song is like an aerobics workout. There is a lead singer and backing vocals together in a question and answer format. The lead singer sings the first verse and then asks questions to the backing vocals. The class could sing along with the backing vocals and mime the actions.

I can't hear you
I can't hear you sing
I can't hear you
I can't hear you sing

Can you sing louder
So I can hear your voice again?
Can you sing louder
So I can hear your voice again?

Can you raise your hands?
   Yes I can!
Can you drink the sea?
   No I can't!
Can you clap your hands?
   Yes I can!
Can you count to three?
   One, two, three!

I can't hear you …

Can you touch your nose?
   Yes I can!
Can you touch the sky?
   No I can't!
Can you move your toes?
   Yes I can!
Can you count to five?
   One, two, three, four, five!

I can't hear you …

Can you touch …

I can't hear you

Songsheet

1 Prediction: Ask students to fold the Songsheet so they can't see the lyric exercise. Students look at the pictures and find the matching phrases. Then you could ask them which of these actions they can do, eg *Can you clap your hands?*, and to demonstrate the actions.
2 **Detail:** Play the song. Students order the pictures as they hear the actions. (Answers: *1H, 2G, 3A, 4E, 5D, 6B, 7F, 8C*)
3 Students unfold the Songsheet and complete the lyric. Play the song again for them to check their answers.
4 **Pronunciation:** Students listen to the difference between the short vowel in *can* and the long vowel in *can't* and try to pronounce them.
5 Students sing with the backing vocals and mime the actions. Later, groups of volunteers could sing the lead vocal to the karaoke version while the rest of the class respond as the backing vocals.
6 Vocabulary: Students could categorize nouns and verbs in the song according to the titles *head*, *arms* or *legs*, eg:
 head: nose, hear, sing, drink
 arms: hands, clap, touch
 legs: toes
Then they could brainstorm more words for these lists, eg:
 head: see, think, ear, mouth, hair, comb, teeth
 arms: fingers, wave, write, draw, type
 legs: knees, run, walk

Grammar page

1 Students do exercise A and then suggest other things that could be included on their ideal penknife.
2 After exercise B, students could say which kind of holiday they would prefer.
3 Exercise C focuses on the form of sentences with *can* and *can't*. Students should realize that they do not need the auxiliaries *do* or *be* with *can*.
4 Exercise D focuses on the meaning of *can*: questions about ability (as practised so far in this unit) or requests. It could be done in pairs with one asking and the other answering.
Note: In English and many other languages, a sentence which looks like a question about ability can function as a request. This is more polite than just using an imperative.

Game page

SMALL GROUPS ACTIVITY
1 Demonstrate this game by giving instructions to the whole class, with and without *please*.
2 When the students have the idea, leave them to play in groups of four or five.

4 I CAN'T HEAR YOU   **Songsheet**

A Match these phrases with the pictures:

count to three   move your toes   drink the sea   touch the sky
raise your hand   count to five   touch your nose clap your hands

B Listen and number the pictures in the correct order.

C Can you complete the song? Listen to check your answers.

I can't hear you, I can't hear you sing **(repeat)**

Can you sing louder, so I can hear your voice again? **(repeat)**

Can you _____? _____!

Can you _____? _____!

Can you _____? _____!

Can you _____? _____!

I can't hear you …

Can you _____? _____!

Can you _____? _____!

Can you _____? _____!

Can you _____? _____!

I can't hear you …

Can you touch …

From **Singing Grammar** by Mark Hancock © Cambridge University Press 1998   **PHOTOCOPIABLE**   27

Grammar page

I CAN'T HEAR YOU **4**

A Look at this penknife. Write at least six things you can do with it.

Example: *You can cut your nails.*

B What can you do on holiday in these places?

Example: *At the beach you can swim.*

in the mountains

at the beach

in a city

C Correct these sentences.

1 Do you can swim?

2 He can't rides a bicycle.

3 I no can remember her name.

4 Can help me you?

5 Can you singing this song?

6 They can't speak English?

7 Can John move his ears.

8 Is he can play the guitar?

D Look at these questions; why are the answers different?

1 Can you speak English?   Yes, I can.

2 Can you open the window, please?
                           Yes, of course.

Give one of the answers for each of these questions.

3 Can you see that bird in the tree?

4 Can you write your name at the top, please?

5 Can you hear that strange noise?

6 Can you play any musical instruments?

7 Can you use a word processor?

8 Can you play your guitar for us, Peter?

9 Can you type this letter for me, please?

10 Can you wait here, please?

From **Singing Grammar** by Mark Hancock © Cambridge University Press 1998   **PHOTOCOPIABLE**

A You can: comb your hair; open bottles; brush your teeth; draw and write; eat; play tapes; listen to music.

B Examples: At the beach you can: swim; surf; sunbathe; read; play volleyball; dive
In the mountains you can: ski; climb; walk; read; watch birds and animals
In a city you can: shop; go to the cinema; go to the disco; sightsee; visit museums

C 1 Can you swim? 2 He can't ride a bicycle. 3 I can't remember her name. 4 Can you help me? 5 Can you sing this song? 6 They can't speak English. 7 Can John move his ears? 8 Can he play the guitar?

D Because 1 is a question about ability and 2 is a request.
3 Yes, I can. 4 Yes, of course. 5 Yes, I can. 6 Yes, I can. 7 Yes, I can. 8 Yes, of course.
9 Yes, of course. 10 Yes, of course.

28

4 I CAN'T HEAR YOU
Game page

Rules

1 Play this game in groups of four or five.

2 One person gives the instructions from this page.
Example: *Can you stand up, please?*

3 If the person says *please*, you must stand up.

4 If the person doesn't say *please*, you must say *No, sorry!*

5 If you do the action when the person doesn't say *please*, or if you do the wrong action, you are 'out'. You sit down and stop playing.

6 The last person 'out' wins the game.

7 Play the game again with a different person giving instructions.

From **Singing Grammar** by Mark Hancock © Cambridge University Press 1998 *PHOTOCOPIABLE*

SECTION ONE ELEMENTARY
5

Grammar
have got

Music
reggae + karaoke

Topic
In this song, a student with exams and a lot of homework is envious of the easy life of an orang-utan in the zoo. The *you* of the song is the orang-utan.

I've got exams in the afternoon
I've got a lot of homework too
I've got a feeling I've got flu
Why can't I be like you?

You've got a tree there in the zoo
You haven't got any work to do
You've got a bunch of bananas too
Why can't I be like you?

You're just an orang-utan
Sitting in your tree all day
Have you got any space for me
Up there in your tree today?

You've got a lot of friends up there
You sit around and you comb your hair
You haven't got any worries and cares
Why can't I be like you?

You're just ...

You're just ...

I've got exams

Songsheet
1 Prediction: Use the picture to elicit as much as possible about the story in the song.
2 Detail: Play the song. Students look at the jumbled words of the lyric. They should listen for these words as the song is in progress. Then ask them to write out the lyric. They can do this using a combination of memory of the song and knowledge of grammar and word order, with help from the commas which denote line endings. Play the song again for them to check their answers.
3 Pronunciation: Students repeat the song line by line. Focus on the linking between words ending in *t* and words beginning with a vowel sound: *got a; lot of; got any*. Students repeat these as if the final consonant belongs to the following word like this: *go ta; lo tof; go tany*.
4 Students sing along to the song. Once they are confident, they could sing to the karaoke version.
5 Ask students to put away the Songsheet before giving them the Grammar page; this is important as exercise A asks them to identify picture differences from memory.

Grammar page
1 Exercise A asks students to identify picture differences from memory. They can take the Songsheet out again to check their answers.
2 Exercise B asks students to decipher a text in which many words are replaced by symbols, in order to identify the person described. They then go on to write a similar text about themselves. These texts could be collected in and redistributed. The reader would then try to identify the classmate who wrote the text.
3 Exercise C is a dialogue-sequencing exercise. It includes language which will be useful for the Game page activity, so ask students in pairs to role-play the dialogue once they've finished and checked their answers.

Game page
SMALL GROUPS ACTIVITY
Preparation: Make two copies of the Game page for every group of three (or four) students. Cut out the cards or provide scissors for the students to do this.
1 Brainstorm names of pop singers or groups and write them on the board.
2 Divide the class into groups of three (or four). Give the cards or card sheets out to the groups and ask them to follow the instructions.

5 I'VE GOT EXAMS **Songsheet**

A Look at the picture. Why is the boy unhappy?

B Listen to the song. Listen in particular for the jumbled words below.

C Put these words in order, using the commas to help you. There are three lines to complete each verse. Then listen to check.

got exams too, a the	I've got _____
afternoon, lot of feeling	I've got _____
a I've flu, in homework	I've got _____
	Why can't I be like you?

a to do, got zoo, of	You've got _____
too, tree the any work in	You've haven't _____
bananas there bunch a	You've got _____
	Why can't I be like you?

You're just an orang-utan
Sitting in your tree all day
Have you got any space for me
Up there in your tree today?

hair, lot got you comb of	You've got _____
a any up there, and friends	You sit _____
around worries your and cares,	You haven't _____
	Why can't I be like you?
	You're just ... (repeat)

From **Singing Grammar** by Mark Hancock © Cambridge University Press 1998   **PHOTOCOPIABLE**   31

Grammar page

I'VE GOT EXAMS **5**

A Can you remember the picture on the Songsheet? Find the differences in this picture. Use *have got* in your answers.

Example: *The boy's got dark hair.*

B Can you understand this writing? Which girl wrote it, A or B?

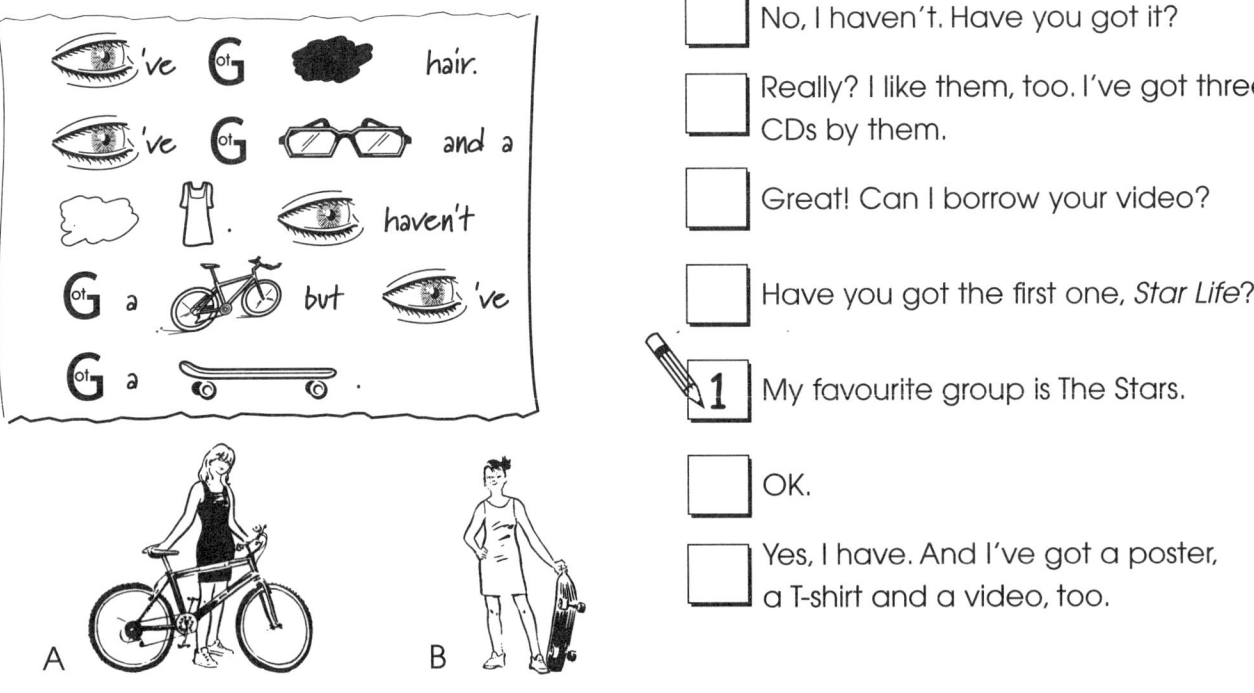

Write a similar text about you.

C Put this dialogue in order.

☐ No, I haven't. Have you got it?

☐ Really? I like them, too. I've got three CDs by them.

☐ Great! Can I borrow your video?

☐ Have you got the first one, *Star Life*?

[1] My favourite group is The Stars.

☐ OK.

☐ Yes, I have. And I've got a poster, a T-shirt and a video, too.

From **Singing Grammar** by Mark Hancock © Cambridge University Press 1998 **PHOTOCOPIABLE**

---

answers

A The boy's got dark hair, a walkman and a bike. He hasn't got any books and he hasn't got a watch. The orang-utan's got two bunches of bananas, sunglasses, a baseball cap and a watch.

B The text describes girl B.

C — My favourite group is The Stars.
— Really? I like them, too. I've got three CDs by them.
— Have you got the first one, *Star Life*?
— No, I haven't. Have you got it?
— Yes, I have. And I've got a poster, a T-shirt and a video, too.
— Great! Can I borrow your video?
— OK.

5 I'VE GOT EXAMS

Game page

Rules

1. Play this game in groups of three or four. Your group will need a set of 24 cards. Each group must choose the names of two different pop singers or groups.

2. Divide the cards into six *families*. Each *family* has a CD, a T-shirt, a poster and a video. Write the names of one singer or group on each set of cards. Then put all the cards together and mix them.

3. The object of the game is to collect *families*.

4. Each player takes two cards.

5. Take turns to ask one of the other players for a card.
   Example: *Michael: Have you got a 'David Star' T-shirt, Fatma?*
   If Fatma's got this card, she gives it to Michael, and Michael can ask again. If Fatma hasn't got this card, Michael takes a card from the table (if there are any left) and it's the next player's turn.

6. If you make a *family*, put it on the table in front of you. The person with most families at the end is the winner.

From **Singing Grammar** by Mark Hancock © Cambridge University Press 1998 **PHOTOCOPIABLE**

SECTION ONE ELEMENTARY

Grammar
irregular past tense verbs

Music
pop + karaoke

Topic
The singer narrates what happened during the day. However, the story is very strange because it is full of contradictions, such as *I ate a cup of tea*. The backing vocals repeat each line after the lead singer.

I woke up this morning
And I got into bed
Then I ate a cup of tea
And drank a slice of bread
Oh, what a crazy day!
Oh, what a crazy day!

I went to the bus stop
And caught the train to school
Then I rode my bicycle
In the swimming pool
Oh, what a crazy day!
Oh, what a crazy day!

Someone broke the telephone
So then I rang my friend
We went to the football field
And swam from end to end
Oh, what a crazy day!
Oh, what a crazy day!

I came home this evening
And watched the radio
I lay down on the ceiling
And read a video
Oh, what a crazy day!
Oh, what a crazy day!

What a crazy day!

Songsheet

1 Gist: Give students the title of the song. Play the song and ask them to listen and explain why it was a crazy day.

2 Detail: Give out the Songsheet and ask students to fold it so they can only see the pictures. Play the song. Students order the pictures. (Answers: *1F, 2D, 3B, 4H, 5E, 6C, 7A, 8G*)

3 Students unfold the Songsheet and order the lines, using the pictures to help them. Alternatively, you could cut the lines of the song out and ask students to put the strips of paper in the right order. Play the song again for them to check their answers.

4 Pronunciation: Ask students to focus on the vowel sound in *bed*. Ask them to find eight more words in the song with this sound. (Answers: *ate, bread, went, then, telephone, friend, end, read*) Point out that *ate* may be pronounced like the number *eight* or as /et/. The past tense of *read* is spelt the same but pronounced like the colour *red*.

5 Students sing along with the backing vocals. Once they are familiar with the song, they could sing to the karaoke version.

6 Extension: Students write more verses for the song with similar contradictions.

Grammar page

1 In exercise A, students circle the verbs in the wordsearch.

2 Exercise B focuses on the negative form of the past simple. The sentences are responses to contradictions in the song.

3 Exercise C asks students to deduce what a person might have done yesterday by looking at the objects in their room. Students should write eight questions. After this exercise, students could ask the questions to each other and give short answers: *Yes, I did/No, I didn't*.

Game page
PAIRS ACTIVITY

1 Give out the Game page and ask students to prepare their questions.

2 Students could role-play the short example dialogue before they begin the activity. Point out the useful language for interviewing: *Excuse me, well, let's see, OK, next question*.

3 Students interview classmates using their questions. Ask them to imagine they are researchers in the street interviewing members of the public, so they should try to be polite.

4 Extension: Students write sentences like these to show the results of their research:
Three people got up before 7 yesterday.
Nobody swam in the sea.

6 WHAT A CRAZY DAY! **Songsheet**

A Listen and put the pictures in order.

B Put the lines of the song in order. Then listen to check.

☐ Then I rode my bicycle
   In the swimming pool

☐ I woke up this morning
   And I got into bed

☐ I came home this evening
   And watched the radio

☐ I lay down on the ceiling
   And read a video

☐ Then I ate a cup of tea
   And drank a slice of bread

☐ I went to the bus stop
   And caught the train to school

☐ Someone broke the telephone
   So then I rang my friend

☐ We went to the football field
   And swam from end to end

From **Singing Grammar** by Mark Hancock © Cambridge University Press 1998 **PHOTOCOPIABLE** 35

Grammar page

WHAT A CRAZY DAY! **6**

A Find the past tense of these verbs:

swim go ring break come watch lie
read catch ride drink wake get eat

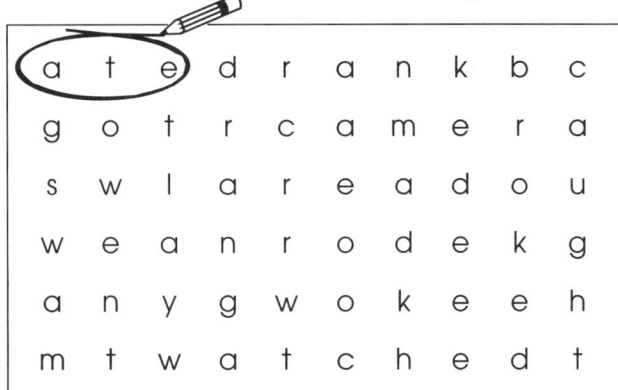

B Complete these sentences with the verbs in exercise A.

1 You didn't _____ into bed, you _____ out of bed!

2 You didn't _____ a slice of bread, you _____ a cup of tea!

3 You didn't _____ a cup of tea, you _____ a slice of bread!

4 You didn't _____ the train to school, you _____ the bus to school!

5 You didn't _____ your bike in the swimming pool, you _____ it in the park!

Write two more similar sentences about the song.

C Look at this room. Can you guess what this person did yesterday? Write questions to ask the person.

Example: *Did you go to the cinema yesterday?*

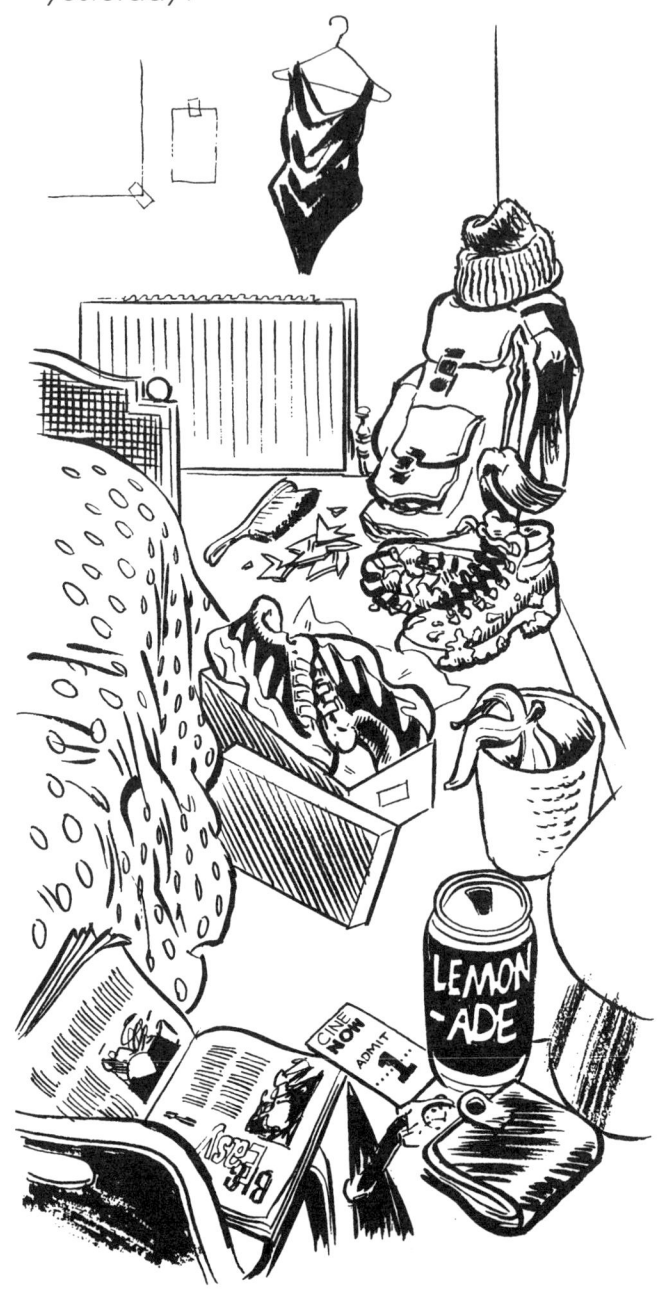

From **Singing Grammar** by Mark Hancock © Cambridge University Press 1998 **PHOTOCOPIABLE**

---

answers

A Across: drank; got; came; read; rode; woke; watched
Down: swam; went; lay; rang; broke; caught

B 1 get; got
2 drink; drank
3 eat; ate
4 catch; caught
5 ride; rode

C Did you: go to the cinema; go swimming; drink lemonade; read a magazine; break a glass; eat a banana; go to the mountains; buy some new trainers?

36

6 WHAT A CRAZY DAY! — Game page

A Choose ten questions and <u>underline</u> one of the options, or think of a new one.
Example:
1 wake up: <u>before 7</u>; after 9; with the alarm clock ...

B Interview four classmates. Begin like this:

Excuse me, I'm doing some research. Could you answer some questions, please?

Yes, of course.

OK, well, did you wake up before 7 o'clock yesterday?

Ehm, let's see ... No, I didn't.

OK, and did you drink tea yesterday?

Yes, I did. I drank two cups of tea in the morning.

OK, next question ...

1 wake up: before 7; after 9; with the alarm clock ...
2 drink: tea; coffee; cola; milk; beer ...
3 ride: a bicycle; a motorbike; a horse; a camel ...
4 come to school: on foot; by car; by bus; by train ...
5 get up: before your sister; before 8; before it was light; early ...
6 go to: the cinema; the shopping centre; school; the disco ...
7 eat: spaghetti; toast; chocolate; a hamburger ...
8 watch: the news; a football match; a video ...
9 read: a newspaper; a book; more than 5 pages; a magazine ...
10 have: a shower; a bath; a walk; a party ...
11 ring: a friend; a relative; anybody ...
12 lie: on the sofa; on the floor; on the carpet ...
13 go: swimming; running; climbing; cycling ...
14 catch: a bus; a train; a plane; a ferry ...
15 break: anything; the law; a rule ...
16 get: anything from the shops; new trainers; a haircut ...
17 eat: a big breakfast; between meals; a big lunch ...
18 swim: in the sea; in a river; in a hotel pool ...
19 go: to the seaside; to the country; to the mountains ...
20 speak: English ...

From **Singing Grammar** by Mark Hancock © Cambridge University Press 1998 **PHOTOCOPIABLE**

SECTION TWO PRE-INTERMEDIATE
7

Grammar
present simple (1st, 3rd person affirmative, negative)

Music
rock + karaoke

Topic
This is an account of daily life from the point of view of an alien in a computer game called *Space invaders*. The space invader addresses *you* (the listener) as a person who likes playing computer games. In the first verse, the alien introduces itself. The account of the daily routine begins in the second verse with *I wake up ...*, and ends in the last verse with *... we go to bed*.

I'm your space invader
And I live behind your screen
I'm your favourite alien
Come and play with me

I wake up in the morning
And I lie in bed and think
I comb my hair and brush my teeth
And then I have a drink

I know you like computer games
You know I like them too
I live in a computer
And there's nothing else to do

I eat fast food for breakfast
And I read a magazine
You switch on your computer
And I jump behind your screen

I stand there with my monster friends
We wave our arms and legs
We move around, you shoot us down
And then we go to bed

I know you like ...

I stand there ...

Space invader

Songsheet

Preparation: Make one copy of the Songsheet for every two students in the class and cut it into Songsheets A and B. Give half the class Songsheet A and the other half Songsheet B. You may want to give sheets A and B to students who are sitting together so they do not have to move for the information-gap activity.

1 Prediction: Ask students to fold the Songsheet so they cannot see the words, and describe the situation in the pictures. Note that the pictures are different on Songsheets A and B. Put elicited and new vocabulary on the board, for example: *screen, alien, computer game* ... Students write down these words. You could allow students A and B to look at each other's pictures at this point.

2 Detail: Play the song. Students listen and tick the words they hear. They can use these words and the pictures to discuss in pairs what the song is about. Note that students with Songsheet A will have to remember the description of picture B from step 1 above (and vice versa).

3 Get feedback from the whole class about the story in the song.

4 Information gap: Students unfold the Songsheet and work with a partner who has the other version of the Songsheet. They should compare the lyrics on their sheets without looking at their partner's sheet. They should make a note of any word which is different on their partner's sheet. (All the words that are different are verbs.)

5 Detail: Play the song. Students listen to identify which word is correct: the word on their sheet or the word on their partner's sheet. They should underline the words they hear. Students check by looking together at the two Songsheets, and correct their own.

6 Pronunciation: Students repeat the song; pause after each line. Focus on linking between words ending in a consonant sound with following words starting in a vowel sound:

space‿invader; and‿I; come‿and; wake‿up; morning‿and; bed‿and; hair‿and; teeth‿and; then‿I; have‿a; live‿in; computer‿and; nothing‿else; breakfast‿and; read‿a; switch‿on; computer‿and; wave‿our‿arms‿and; move‿around; shoot‿us; down‿and.

Ask students to repeat these as if the final consonant belongs to the following word like this: *spa sinvader; an dI*.

7 Students sing along to the song. Once they are familiar with it, they could sing to the karaoke version.

Grammar page

1 In exercise A, students write four sentences from the jumbled words and phrases. Make sure that there is agreement between subject and verb.

2 Students could extend exercise B and suggest other things the astronauts do or don't do.

3 Exercises C and D focus on daily routines. You could use D as an example of what the students have to do in the Game page activity.

Game page
SMALL GROUPS ACTIVITY

Preparation: Make one copy of the Game page for every group of three or four students in the class. Cut out the cards to make a pack, or provide scissors for the students to do this. For each pack of cards, there is also a rules sheet, which will be left over when the cards have been cut out. Note that some cards are blank and students have to decide on a name to write on them.

1 Take one card yourself, and begin to describe the daily routine of the person or thing on the card. Ask the students to guess what is on your card.

2 Divide the students into groups. Give each group a pack of cards and the rules sheet. Leave them to play the game.

7 SPACE INVADER — Songsheet

Songsheet A

A List words you can use to describe this picture. Then listen to the song and tick (✓) the listed words you hear.

B Find a partner with Songsheet B. <u>Don't</u> look at your partner's sheet. Compare your lyrics and find ten differences. Make a note if your partner's word is different.
Example: A: *My next line is 'And I work behind your screen'.*
B: *OK, that's different. On my lyric, it's 'live', not 'work'.*

I'm your space invader
And I work behind your screen
I'm your favourite alien
Come and play with me

I get up in the morning
And I lie in bed and think
I comb my hair and brush my teeth
And then I have a drink

I think you like computer games
You know I like them too
I live in a computer
And there's nothing else to do

I have fast food for breakfast
And I read a magazine
You switch on your computer
And I jump behind your screen

I stand there with my monster friends
We wave our arms and legs
We turn around, you shoot us down
And then we go to bed

C Listen to the song. Which of your words were correct? Which of your partner's words were correct? Correct your lyric.

Songsheet B

A List words you can use to describe this picture. Then listen to the song and tick (✓) the listed words you hear.

B Find a partner with Songsheet A. <u>Don't</u> look at your partner's sheet. Compare your lyrics and find ten differences. Make a note if your partner's word is different.
Example: B: *My next line is 'Go and play with me'.*
A: *OK, that's different. On my lyric, it's 'come' not 'go'.*

I'm your space invader
And I live behind your screen
I'm your favourite alien
Go and play with me

I wake up in the morning
And I lie in bed and think
I comb my hair and clean my teeth
And then I have a drink

I know you like computer games
You know I like them too
I work in a computer
And there's nothing else to do

I eat fast food for breakfast
And I read a magazine
You turn on your computer
And I jump behind your screen

I sit there with my monster friends
We wave our arms and legs
We move around, you shoot us down
And then we go to bed

C Listen to the song. Which of your words were correct? Which of your partner's words were correct? Correct your lyric.

From **Singing Grammar** by Mark Hancock © Cambridge University Press 1998

Grammar page

SPACE INVADER 7

A Make four sentences from these words and phrases:

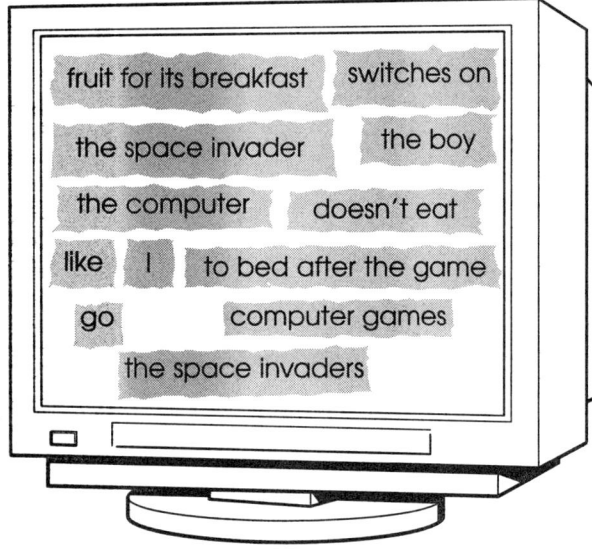

fruit for its breakfast | switches on | the space invader | the boy | the computer | doesn't eat | like | I | to bed after the game | go | computer games | the space invaders

B Look at this room in a spaceship. Write down five things the astronauts do.
Example: *They listen to music.*

Write down five things the astronauts don't do.
(The spaceship doesn't have these things: a swimming pool bicycles fresh fruit a piano newspapers a telephone.)
Example: *They don't read newspapers.*

C Read this information about Derek Different.

Derek Different gets up at five o'clock in the morning. He has a bath, then he has salad for breakfast. He goes to school by skateboard. He stays at school for two hours and then he goes home. He plays computer games all afternoon. For dinner he eats carrots and cornflakes. He sleeps on the kitchen table.

Are you the same as Derek? Write five sentences.
Example: *I don't get up at five o'clock; I get up at half past seven ...*

D Can you guess this person's job?

I get up very early. I have a big breakfast and then I go out to milk the cows. After that I feed the animals. Sometimes, I drive the tractor in the fields. I watch television in the evening and I go to bed early.

From **Singing Grammar** by Mark Hancock © Cambridge University Press 1998 **PHOTOCOPIABLE**

---

answers

A The space invader doesn't eat fruit for its breakfast.
The boy switches on the computer.
The space invaders go to bed after the game.
I like computer games.

B They drink space cola.
They play table tennis.
They watch videos.
They take photographs.
They play cards.
They don't swim.
They don't ride bicycles.
They don't eat fresh fruit.
They don't play the piano.
They don't talk on the phone.

D A farmer

40

7 SPACE INVADER — Game page

Rules

1 Play this game in groups of three or four. Put the cards face down in the middle.

2 One player takes a card and describes the daily routine of the person or thing on the card. (On some cards, the player has to write the name of a famous person or an animal and describe their routine.) The other players guess what is written on the card. (A player may take a second card if he/she thinks the first is too difficult.)

3 The first player to guess wins the card. Then it's the next player's turn to take a card.

4 When all the cards are finished, count your cards. The player with most cards wins.

From **Singing Grammar** by Mark Hancock © Cambridge University Press 1998 **PHOTOCOPIABLE**

SECTION TWO PRE-INTERMEDIATE

Grammar
countable and uncountable nouns, quantifiers

Music
pop + karaoke

Topic
In this song, a person wakes up hungry in the night and goes to the kitchen to find something to eat. However, in the fridge, there isn't anything she wants to eat.

You wake up in the night
And you're lying on your back
You feel a little hungry
It's time for a snack

You go down to the kitchen
And you switch on the light
You open the fridge
And this is what you find
This is what you find ...

You find a little cheese
But it isn't very nice
There are a few frozen peas
There's a lot of cooked rice

You try to make a sandwich
But there isn't much bread
There isn't any butter
So you just go back to bed
You just go back to bed

Well, you're dreaming of a pizza
But there aren't any tomatoes
And there isn't any tuna
There are just a few potatoes

*

You try ...

And dream of a pizza
You dream of a pizza

Dream of a pizza

Songsheet

Preparation: Make one copy of the Songsheet for each student. Alternatively, make one copy for each pair of students and cut the lines of the jumbled lyric into strips for the students to put in order.

1 Prediction: Tell students they will hear a song called *Dream of a pizza* about the picture. Ask students to fold the Songsheet (if you haven't cut the lyric into strips) so they can only see the beginning of the song and the picture. Ask them to suggest how the song will continue.

2 Gist: Play the song and ask students to identify the items in the picture as they hear them.

3 Students unfold the Songsheet and look at the jumbled lyric. Alternatively, give out the strips of paper containing the lyric. Play the song again and ask them to order the lines. Pause where you see the asterisk (*) in the lyric to avoid confusing the students with the repetition of the verse *You try to make a sandwich ...*

4 Pronunciation: Focus on the pronunciation of the contractions *aren't* and *isn't*. Also note linking in *there are a few*. Because *there* and *are* are followed by a vowel (the indefinite article), the /r/ is pronounced to separate the two words (the /r/ need not be pronounced in *there* and *are* normally). Because *isn't* is followed by a word beginning with a vowel, the final /t/ links to the following word like this:
isn tany.

5 Students sing along to the song. Once they know the song, they could sing to the karaoke version.

6 Extension: Students could write more verses for the song and sing their verses to the karaoke version. Here are some rhymes you could provide to help them:
cheese/peas; sweet/meat/eat; cherry/berry; rice/nice/ice; lamb/jam/ham; tomato/potato (but note the difference of the 2nd vowel in British English); *tangerines/beans; sandwiches/cabbages/sausages/oranges; cake/steak/awake; toast/taste* (different vowel)
Alternatively, students could use similar sounding words even if they do not rhyme, eg *grapes/cakes*.

7 Ask students to put away the Songsheet before giving them the Grammar page; this is important for the memory game in exercise B.

Grammar page

1 After exercise A you could ask students to put the possible quantifiers after each sentence beginning:
  There is: *some, a lot of, a little, no*
  There are: *some, a lot of, a few, no*
  There isn't/Is there: *any, much*
  There are/Are there: *any, many*

Note: Although other forms such as *Are there some ...* can be used for emphasis, this unit focuses on the forms without emphasis first.

2 Students check their answers for exercise B by looking again at the Songsheet picture.

3 Exercise C helps prepare students for the Game page activity.

Game page

PAIRS ACTIVITY

Preparation: For every pair of students in the class, get a copy of the Game page and a dice. You may want to cut off the answers at the bottom of the page, or ask students to fold the page back.

1 Divide the class into pairs or groups of three. Give each a Game page and dice.
2 The rules are given on the Game page, but you could demonstrate how to win squares by rolling the dice, saying the number and asking students to say which squares on the board you could win with that number.

8 DREAM OF A PIZZA **Songsheet**

A Look at the first lines of the song and the picture. How do you think the song will continue?

> You wake up in the night
> And you're lying on your back
> You feel a little hungry
> It's time for a snack
> You go down to the kitchen
> And you switch on the light
> You open the fridge
> And this is what you find ...

B Listen and put these lines in order. Then listen to check.

☐ You try to make a sandwich

☐ Well, you're dreaming of a pizza

☐ But it isn't very nice

☐ But there isn't much bread

☐ There are just a few potatoes

☐ And there isn't any tuna

☐ There isn't any butter

[1] You find a little cheese

☐ So you just go back to bed
    You just go back to bed

☐ There's a lot of cooked rice

☐ But there aren't any tomatoes

☐ There are a few frozen peas

From **Singing Grammar** by Mark Hancock © Cambridge University Press 1998 *PHOTOCOPIABLE*

Grammar page

DREAM OF A PIZZA **8**

A Finish these sentences. Use some of these words:

some   no   a lot of   a few   a little   any   many   much

1 There's _____
2 There are _____
3 There isn't _____
4 There aren't _____
5 Is there _____ ?
6 Are there _____ ?

B Can you remember the picture on the Songsheet? What is different in this picture?
Example: Songsheet picture: *There isn't much cheese.*
This picture: *There's a lot of cheese.*

C Match the beginnings and endings of these sentences:

There's — some milk.
There's — a few tomatoes.
There are — much fruit?
There are — some milk.
There isn't — any apples?
There aren't — some eggs.
Is there — a little cheese.
Are there — many grapes.

From **Singing Grammar** by Mark Hancock © Cambridge University Press 1998   **PHOTOCOPIABLE**

answers

B Differences in the picture on this page:
There's a lot of butter.
There isn't any rice.
There's a lot of cheese.
There are a lot of peas.
There are some tomatoes and carrots.
There aren't any potatoes.
There's a lot of bread.
There's a lot of tuna.
There's some orange juice.
There are a few eggs.

C There's: some milk; a little cheese.
There are: a few tomatoes; some eggs.
There isn't: any steak.
There aren't: many grapes.
Is there: much fruit?
Are there: any apples?

44

8 DREAM OF A PIZZA **Game page**

Rules

1 Play this game in pairs; you need a dice.

2 To win the game, you must get more points than the other player. To get points, you must get lines with four squares like this:

a few tomatoes.	much fruit?	some milk.	any apples?

3 Take turns to throw the dice. Each number is the beginning of a sentence like this:
 1 = There's   4 = There aren't
 2 = There are   5 = Is there
 3 = There isn't   6 = Are there
So if you throw 1, find a square that makes a sentence beginning with *There's*.
Example: *There's some milk.*

4 If you correctly find a square, draw something in it to remember it is your square. One player could use a nought (0), the other a cross (X). If you can't find a square to finish your sentence, miss a turn.

5 When there are no more empty squares, count your points: one point for every line of four. For example, this is four points:

any bananas?	a little fish.	a few fish.	any potatoes?	much potato.
much time.	any chicken?	a little oil.	any news?	a lot of traffic.
many cakes.	a lot of teabags.	some bread.	a few lemons.	any carrots.
a lot of wine.	much tea?	a lot of rice.	any sugar?	a little salad.

any steak.	a few tomatoes.	much fruit?	some milk.	any apples?	some eggs.
a little cheese.	many grapes.	no milk.	a few peas.	any money.	many people.
much water?	any bananas?	a little fish.	a few fish.	any potatoes?	much potato.
some biscuits.	much time.	any chicken?	a little oil.	any news?	a lot of traffic.
any cake?	many cakes.	a lot of teabags.	some bread.	a few lemons.	any carrots.
much homework	a lot of wine.	much tea?	a lot of rice.	any sugar?	a little salad.

From **Singing Grammar** by Mark Hancock © Cambridge University Press 1998 **PHOTOCOPIABLE**

---

answers

1 some milk; a little cheese; no milk; a little fish; a little oil; a lot of traffic; some bread; a lot of wine; a lot of rice; a little salad
2 a few tomatoes; some eggs; a few peas; a few fish; some biscuits; a lot of teabags; a few lemons; some milk
3 any money; much potato; much time; much homework; any steak
4 many grapes; many people; many cakes; any carrots
5 much fruit? much water? any chicken? any news? any cake? much tea? any sugar?
6 any apples? any bananas? any potatoes?

45

SECTION TWO PRE-INTERMEDIATE

Blue train

Grammar
adjective order

Music
rock and roll + karaoke

Topic
This song is about a traveller returning home after a long time away. The things mentioned such as the train, the track and the hills are each mentioned three times, with one new descriptive adjective added each time.

I'm sitting on a blue train
    An old blue train
    An old blue express train
Going down a steel track
    A long steel track
    A long steel railway track
Passing through green hills
    Big green hills
    Beautiful big green hills
On my way back home
    Home sweet home

I'm sitting on a white plane
    A fast white plane
    A fast white passenger plane
Flying through the blue sky
    The wide blue sky
    The beautiful wide blue sky
High above the deep sea
    The deep green sea
    The wonderful deep green sea
On my way back home
    Home sweet home

I'm on my way back home
I've been away too long

I'm sitting on a blue train
    An old blue train
    An old blue express train

Songsheet

1 Ask students to fold the Songsheet and look only at the pictures. Play the song. Students identify things in the pictures mentioned in the song.

2 Detail: Students unfold the Songsheet and listen again, putting the jumbled words in order. There will not be enough time for them to write out the unjumbled words while the song is playing, so advise them to put their pens down while listening and try to remember the order. Play the song again for students to complete/check the exercise.

3 Pronunciation: Note how words with a final consonant link to following words starting with another consonant. The final consonant may not be fully pronounced; the /t/ in *white plane* for example. The /t/ here may be pronounced as a glottal stop. It would be very difficult and artificial-sounding to pronounce this /t/ fully. Ask students to repeat lines of the song after you or by listening to the song again.

4 Students sing along to the song. Once they know the song, they could sing to the karaoke version.

5 Vocabulary: Students list words from the song under the following categories: *vehicles; geographical features; colours; size; opinions*. They could then brainstorm other words to add to their lists.

6 Extension: Students could write more verses for the song and sing them to the karaoke version.

Grammar page

1 Exercises A and B concern adjective order.
Note: With adjective order, it is probably easier for students to get a feel for it, rather than try to memorize a long list of rules. However, you may want to use the following analysis in exercise A if your students require explicit rules: nearest the noun is its class, eg *express train* is a class, or type, of train. The colour words come before the class. Words about age (*old*), size (*long*) and speed (*fast*) come before the colour word. The first adjective in the group is a subjective opinion, for example *beautiful*.
2 Exercise B is preparation for the Game page activity. It needs to be done in conjunction with the gapped rules on the Game page.

Game page

SMALL GROUPS ACTIVITY

Preparation: Make one copy of the Game page for every group of three or four students. Cut out the cards or provide scissors for the students to do this. The completed rules sheet will be left over when the cards have been cut out.
1 Divide the class into groups of three or four and give each group a set of cards and a rule sheet.
2 Students look again at the pictures on the Grammar page to see how to play the game: players hide their cards with their arm or hand. Players must make phrases. The phrases must cross.
3 Go round the tables of each group during the game to check that their phrases are correct.

9 BLUE TRAIN — Songsheet

A Listen to the song. What do you hear about the train and the plane?

B Put the jumbled words in order on the two lines of each verse. Then listen and check.

I'm sitting on a blue train
blue an express train blue
old train an old

_____
_____

Going down a steel track
steel a steel railway track
a long track long

_____
_____

Passing through green hills
hills green big big hills
green beautiful

_____
_____

On my way back home
Home sweet home

I'm sitting on a white plane
white white plane passenger
fast plane a fast a

_____
_____

Flying through the blue sky
sky sky blue wide the
beautiful the blue wide

_____
_____

High above the deep sea
green deep the sea the sea
wonderful green deep

_____
_____

On my way back home
Home sweet home

I'm on my way back home
I've been away too long

I'm sitting ... express train

From **Singing Grammar** by Mark Hancock © Cambridge University Press 1998   PHOTOCOPIABLE   47

Grammar page

BLUE TRAIN 9

A Look at the order of the adjectives in these lines from the song:

An old blue express train
A long steel railway track
Beautiful big green hills
A fast white passenger plane
The beautiful wide blue sky
The wonderful deep green sea

Put these words in a similar order:

1 green / guitar / new / electric / a
2 big / shopping / a / bag / plastic
3 little / roller / ugly / skates
4 racket / beautiful / new / tennis / the / red
5 ship / old / sailing / a / wonderful
6 little / boat / fishing / the / pretty
7 fast / a / black / car / sports

8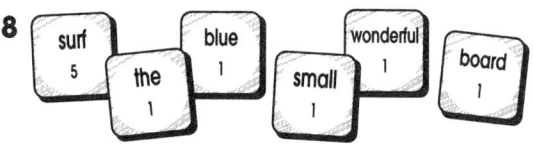

B These students are playing a game. You can help. Look at the Rules on the Game page.

1 It's Jorge's turn. This is his hand. What can he do? How many points will he get?

2 Sonja is putting the card here. Is this correct? Does Sonja miss her turn, or can she try again?

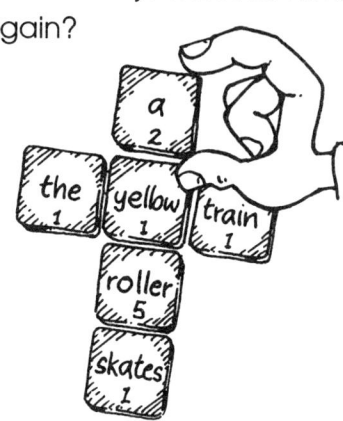

3 It's Toshi's turn. This is his hand. Can he finish all these cards? If he does, how many points will he win?

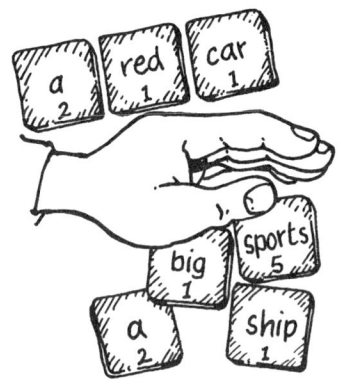

From **Singing Grammar** by Mark Hancock © Cambridge University Press 1998 **PHOTOCOPIABLE**

---

answers

A
1 a new green electric guitar
2 a big plastic shopping bag
3 ugly little roller skates
4 the beautiful new red tennis racket
5 a wonderful old sailing ship
6 the pretty little fishing boat
7 a fast black sports car
8 the wonderful small blue surf board

B
1 His best play would be *an unusual long boat* = 8 points
2 It's a mistake because the phrase is plural. She misses her turn.
3 He can finish his cards, placing them vertically: *a sports car, a big ship* = 9 points

9 BLUE TRAIN

Game page

Rules

What are the rules of the game? Look carefully at the pictures on the Grammar page.

1 Each player takes _____ cards. Leave the rest of the cards on the _____ .

2 Put cards down to make phrases. The phrases can cross. When you make a phrase, add the _____ on each card you have put down to find how many _____ you get.

3 If you make a mistake, you miss your _____ .

4 After your turn, take more _____ from the table so you have four again.

5 In this game, you can't have two _____ of the same type together, for example, *a **blue red** train*. This sounds very strange!

6 If you can't make a _____, miss a turn.

7 You can make more than one phrase in your turn. You can put a word in the middle of a phrase, eg *a train*; you can add *blue* to make *a blue train*.

8 When there are no cards left, count the points to find the _____ .

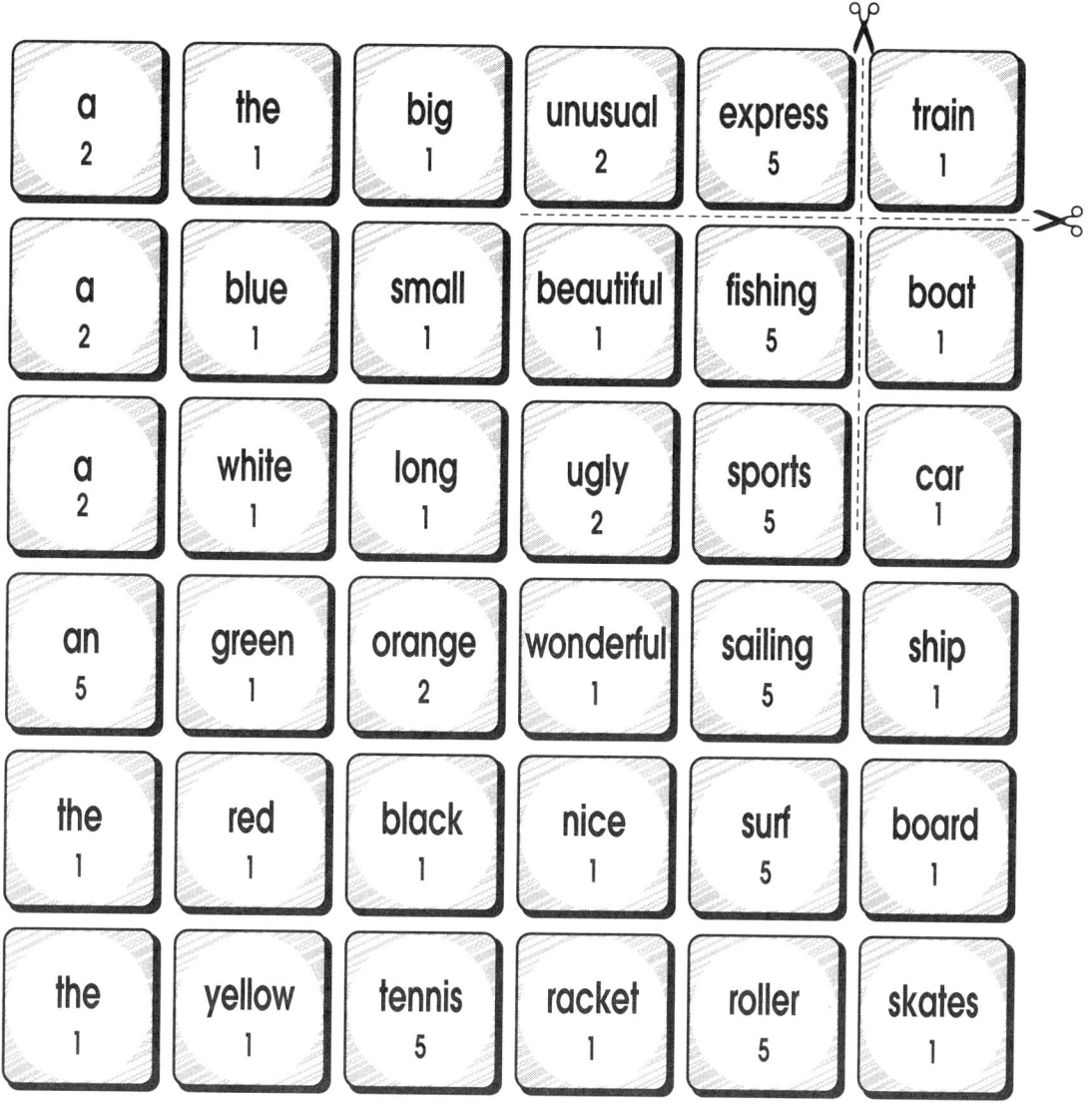

answers

1 four; table 2 numbers; points 3 turn 4 cards 5 adjectives 6 phrase 8 winner

From **Singing Grammar** by Mark Hancock © Cambridge University Press 1998 **PHOTOCOPIABLE** 49

SECTION TWO PRE-INTERMEDIATE — 10

Grammar
comparatives

Music
🔊 rock ballad + karaoke

Topic
The singer addresses another boy, who is a rival for the love of a girl. The singer makes a contrast between the great advantages the other boy has and the fact that the girl prefers the singer; this contrast is marked by the word *but*.

You want the same girl as me
You think you're better than me
But it's easy to see she loves me

You've got more money than me
You're better looking than me
But it's easy to see she loves me

I love her and she loves me
I'm happier than the birds in the trees
You've got money but can't you see
You can't take her love from me

Your work is better than mine
Your marks are higher than mine
But it's easy to see she loves me

You're more attractive than me
But not as happy as me
Because it's easy to see she loves me

I love her ...

Happier than the birds

Songsheet
1 Prediction: Ask students to fold the Songsheet so they can only see the pictures. Explain that the pictures represent a song and ask students to brainstorm words they <u>might</u> hear in the song, eg *me, you, money, girl, love, marks, cry*. Write these on the board.
2 🔊 **Detail:** Play the song. Students listen for the words listed on the board.
3 🔊 Students unfold the Songsheet and write the lines of the lyric. They should do this from memory, with help from the capitals and commas and using their knowledge of grammar. Play the song again for them to check their answers.
4 Pronunciation: Focus on the pronunciation of the weak forms *as* and *than*. In both, the vowel is reduced to a schwa /ə/.
5 🔊 Students sing along to the song. Once they know the song, they could sing to the karaoke version.
6 🔊 **Extension:** Students could write more verses of their own and sing them to the karaoke version of the song.

Grammar page
1 You could set a time limit for exercise A and announce that the student with most sentences will be the winner. You may want to make sure that students use various comparative forms by suggesting they use at least three *-er* and at least three *as* forms.
2 Exercises B and C are puzzles which prepare the student for the Game page activity. Again, you may want to enforce the use of the two comparative forms. After checking the key for exercise B, you could ask students to write the paragraph in full.
Statistics for C: Pacific — 165,384,000 km^2; Atlantic — 82,217,000 km^2; Indian — 73,481,000 km^2; Arctic — 14,056,000 km^2

Game page
PAIRS ACTIVITY
1 Give one copy of the Game page to each student, and ask them to play the game in pairs.
2 Ask them to read the rules carefully. Then demonstrate. Put the words of A in a secret order yourself and invite students to ask questions to find the order.
Statistics for B: Everest — 8,848 m; Aconcagua — 6,960 m; Kilimanjaro — 5,895 m; Blanc — 4,810 m
Statistics for D: Nile — 6,695 km; Amazon — 6,570 km; Mississippi — 3,779 km; Danube — 2,850 km
3 Extension: Students could think of their own groups of four words to play this game with, eg size of animal, size of city.

10 HAPPIER THAN THE BIRDS — Songsheet

A You will hear a song called *Happier than the birds* about the people in the pictures. Predict what the song is about.

B Listen and check your predictions.

C Put these words in order, using the capitals and commas to help you. There are two lines to complete each verse. Then listen to check.

the	better	You want
than me,	you're	same
You think	girl	as me,

But it's easy to see she loves me

You've	looking	You're
than me,	better	got
more	than me,	money

But it's easy to see she loves me

I love her and she loves me
I'm happier than the birds in the trees
You've got money but can't you see
You can't take her love from me

than mine,	higher	are
Your	work is	marks
better	than mine,	Your

But it's easy to see she loves me

You're	as happy	than
more	as me,	But
attractive	not	me,

Because it's easy to see she loves me

I love her ...

From **Singing Grammar** by Mark Hancock © Cambridge University Press 1998 **PHOTOCOPIABLE** 51

Grammar page

HAPPIER THAN THE BIRDS **10**

A Find as many differences as you can between these two pictures. Write sentences about picture B. Use *-er*, *as* or *more*.

Example: *The bag is smaller.*
The boy's hair isn't as long.

B Put the four *Transport* words in the boxes according to the text.

TRANSPORT
walking   a bicycle   a train   a plane

1 ✎ a train	2	3	4

1 is faster than 2 but it isn't as fast as 3. 4 isn't as fast as 1 and 2 isn't as fast as 4.

C Write a similar text for the four *Oceans*. First write a secret order for the words. Then write sentences about the order. Check that it is possible to solve the puzzle from your text. Then give your puzzle to a classmate to do.

OCEANS
the Arctic Ocean   the Indian Ocean   the Atlantic   the Pacific

From **Singing Grammar** by Mark Hancock © Cambridge University Press 1998   **PHOTOCOPIABLE**

A The jacket is darker.
The girl's calculation isn't as easy.
The map is smaller and lower.
The boy's pencil is longer.
The boy is happier.
The footballer is taller.
The ball is nearer the goal.
The goal isn't as wide.
The trees are taller.
It's five minutes later.

B 1 a train 2 walking 3 a plane 4 a bicycle

10 HAPPIER THAN THE BIRDS — Game page

Rules

1 Play this game in pairs.

2 Player A writes the four *Animals* words in the boxes in a different order. Don't let player B see your words!

3 Player B asks questions to discover the secret order.
Example: *Is 1 bigger than 2?*
Player A can only answer *yes* or *no*.

4 Player A counts player B's questions. When player B has found the answer, player A writes the total number of questions on the line below the box.

5 Now it is player B's turn to write a secret order for the four *Mountains*. Player A asks questions.

6 The player who asks fewer questions is the winner.

A ANIMALS

a whale   an elephant   a horse   a dog   BIG →

1	2	3	4

Questions asked: _____

B MOUNTAINS

Mont Blanc   Kilimanjaro   Aconcagua   Everest   HIGH →

1	2	3	4

Questions asked: _____

C ACCOMMODATION

camping   a youth hostel   bed & breakfast   a hotel   Expensive →

1	2	3	4

Questions asked: _____

D RIVERS

the Danube   the Mississippi   the Amazon   the Nile   LONG →

1	2	3	4

Questions asked: _____

From **Singing Grammar** by Mark Hancock © Cambridge University Press 1998

SECTION TWO PRE-INTERMEDIATE

Grammar
would like to do/like doing

Music
calypso + karaoke

Topic
This song tells the words and thoughts of a person called Chris who is calling their ex-boy/girlfriend. Chris would like to start up the relationship again and invites Toni out to talk about it. Note that the names *Chris* and *Toni* can be male or female.

I'd like to see you again
I'd like to be in love again

Would you like to
Go out with me tonight?
Won't you please
Give me one more chance?
I'd like to tell you I still love you
Please say that you still love me too

I'd like to ...

I'd like to

Songsheet

1 Prediction: Give out the Songsheet and ask students to read the dialogue and decide the names of the boy and the girl. Ask them to say <u>why</u> they think Toni/Chris is a boy/girl.

2 Detail: Explain that the underlined parts of the dialogue (as well as the words in the thought bubbles) are in the song. Play the song. Students listen and number the underlined parts in the correct order. Play the song again for them to check their answers.

3 Pronunciation: Focus on the pronunciation of the contraction *I'd* and the weak form of *to*.

4 Play the song and ask students to sing along. You could ask students to copy the song from their Songsheet to make it easier to sing from. Once they know the song, they could sing to the karaoke version.

5 Extension: You could ask students in pairs to read out the dialogue on the Songsheet. Point out the typical pessimism of the greetings *not too bad* and *can't complain*. Then students could suggest how the conversation continues. They could also suggest how the relationship between Chris and Toni broke up in the first place.

Grammar page

1 Exercise A asks students to identify the difference in meaning between *like doing* for general taste and *would like to do* for a specific preference. Point out the difference in time references: *at weekends* (general); *at the weekend* (specific).
Note: *Like* to express general taste may be followed by the gerund or infinitive with little change in meaning. These exercises assume that it is best to teach *like* + *gerund* first, because this pattern can be more generalized for affection verbs (*like, enjoy*, etc).
2 Exercises B and C provide further practice in manipulating these forms.
3 Exercises D and E highlight the difference between *like doing* for something a person already does and *would like to do* for a hypothetical situation. Students may need to ask their partner questions before preparing their questionnaire in E. For example, they cannot ask *Do you like having three brothers?* if they do not know about their partner's family. They would have to ask their partner *Have you got any brothers or sisters?* first.
4 You could ask students to write a profile of the person they interviewed.

Game page
PAIRS ACTIVITY

1 Give each student a copy of the Game page and ask them to read the rules.
2 Demonstrate the game. Put a coin on a square of the map (without letting students see it). Students make sentences to give the coordinates of squares on the map. Their sentences should be true. For example, if *I like staying in bed late on Sundays* is not true for them, they should say *I don't like staying in bed late on Sundays*. Check students know all the negative forms during your demonstration: *I wouldn't like ... I don't like ... I don't want ... I don't enjoy ...*
3 Continue the demonstration until one student guesses the right square. Then leave them to play the game in pairs. Early finishers can repeat the game.

11 I'D LIKE TO — Songsheet

A Read this telephone conversation. Which do you think is Toni — the girl or the boy? Whose thoughts are they?

Toni: Hello, Toni Smith here.

Chris: Eh, hi Toni, it's me.

Toni: Oh, hi Chris, how are you?

Chris: Oh, not too bad. And you?

Toni: I can't complain. Long time no see, eh?

Chris: Yeah, I know. Look, [1] <u>I'd like to see you again</u>, Toni. [ ] <u>Would you like to go out with me tonight?</u>

Toni: Well, eh, I don't know …

Chris: Well, you see, [ ] <u>I'd like to tell you</u> something, ehm … <u>I still love you</u>, Toni.

Toni: Look, Chris, I don't think this is a very good idea …

Chris: Come on Toni, I know I was wrong, but [ ] <u>won't you please give me one more chance?</u> Let's go to the cinema or something …

B Listen to the song. Number the underlined parts above in the correct order. Then listen to check.

From **Singing Grammar** by Mark Hancock © Cambridge University Press 1998 PHOTOCOPIABLE 55

Grammar page

I'D LIKE TO **11**

A Read what Sylvia says and answer the questions.

> Generally I like going out on Friday nights but tonight I'm tired and I'd like to stay at home.

1 What does Sylvia want to do tonight?

2 What does Sylvia normally do on Friday nights?

3 What is the difference between these two sentences?
   I like going out.   I'd like to go out.

B Read the Data Profile about Sylvia and answer the questions.

Data Profile	
Nationality:	Canadian
Home:	Montreal
Age:	16
Hair:	blonde
Learning:	Spanish
Brothers/sisters:	2 brothers

1 Which sentence could Sylvia say?
   I like being sixteen years old.
   I'd like to be sixteen years old.

2 Which question could you ask Sylvia?
   Do you like living in London?
   Would you like to live in London?

3 Write four more questions with Would you like ...? and four more with Do you like ...? to ask Sylvia.

C Write one of these at the beginning of each sentence and put the verb in the correct form:

I'd   I   Would you   Do you

1 _____ like _____ (go) to the cinema sometimes.

2 _____ like _____ (go) out at weekends?

3 _____ like _____ (sleep) for a while? You look tired.

4 _____ like _____ (eat) something: I'm hungry.

5 _____ like _____ (drink) tea in the mornings?

6 _____ like _____ (stay) in bed late on Sundays.

7 _____ like _____ (go) out with me this Sunday?

8 _____ like _____ (go) out this evening.

D Use the prompts to write a dialogue between Chris and Toni in the disco.

Chris: Dance?
Toni: No / not like / dance to heavy rock
Chris: OK, drink?
Toni: No / tired / go home

E Find a partner in the class. Prepare at least four questions and then interview your partner.

From **Singing Grammar** by Mark Hancock © Cambridge University Press 1998 **PHOTOCOPIABLE**

---

answers

A 1 Sylvia wants to stay at home. 2 Sylvia normally goes out. 3 *I like* is followed by the *-ing* form of the verb and is used to talk about general likes or tastes. *I'd like* is followed by the infinitive with *to* and is used to talk about a present want or desire.

B 1 I like being sixteen years old.
2 Would you like to live in London?
3 Examples: Do you like being Canadian? Would you like to be Mexican? Do you like having blonde hair? Would you like to have dark hair? Do you like learning Spanish? Would you like to learn German? Do you like having two brothers? Would you like to have sisters?

C 1 I like going 2 Do you like going 3 Would you like to sleep 4 I'd like to eat 5 Do you like drinking 6 I like staying 7 Would you like to go 8 I'd like to go

D Chris: Would you like to dance?
Toni: Well, no, I don't like dancing to heavy rock.
Chris: OK, do you want a drink?
Toni: No, I'm tired, I'd like to go home.

56

11 I'D LIKE TO

Game page

Rules

1 Play this game in pairs.

2 Take a small coin and put it in one square on the island. Don't let your partner see where it is!

3 Try to find which square your partner's coin is in; take turns to ask if the coin is in a square.

4 To ask about a square, make a <u>true</u> sentence. Start the sentences with the words on the left of the map. Continue the sentence with the words above the map. Finish all your sentences with *on Sundays* or *this Sunday*. You can make the sentence negative.
Example: top right square = *I wouldn't like to do my homework this Sunday.*

5 If your partner says the square with your coin, you say *Yes, well done!* If your partner says the square next to the square with the coin, say *Near!* If your partner says a square far from your coin, say *Nothing!*

6 If your partner makes a grammar mistake, say *Incorrect sentence!*

7 The first person to find the coin is the winner.

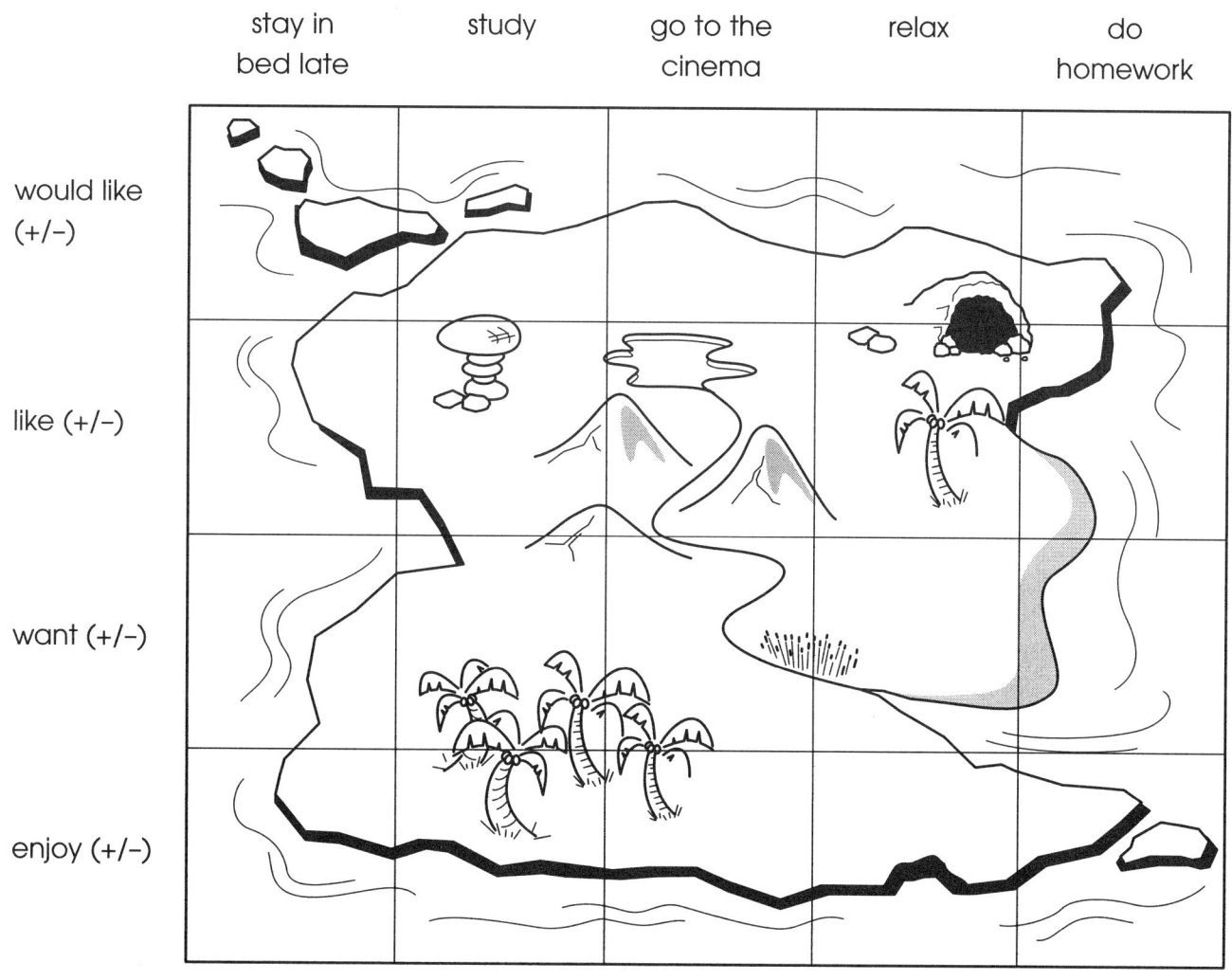

From **Singing Grammar** by Mark Hancock © Cambridge University Press 1998

SECTION TWO PRE-INTERMEDIATE

Grammar
past continuous/past simple

Music
pop + karaoke

Topic
In this song, the singer remembers with nostalgia the beginning of a romance. The singer addresses the loved one, but perhaps only in his thoughts. The song has a repeated pattern of problems and solutions: *I was feeling down/you made me feel OK; I was trying to find the words to say/you turned and smiled; it began to rain/we went to a cafe.*

I was walking down the street one day
When I saw you
Yeah you really took my breath away
Nothing I could do

I was feeling down
You made me feel OK
And I remember to this day
The way you looked at me
The way you made me feel

When I saw you on the street that day
My heart went wild
I was trying to find the words to say
When you turned and smiled

We were standing there
When it began to rain
So we went to a cafe
We walked into that room
And stayed all afternoon

I was walking

Songsheet

1 Prediction: Ask students to fold the Songsheet so they can only see the questions and pictures. Students say as much as they can about the song from the questions and pictures. They may be able to answer most of the questions correctly.

2 Detail: Play the song. Students note/check answers to as many of the questions as possible. If there are any questions they could not answer, ask them to come back to them later.

3 Students unfold the Songsheet and play this text completion game: they call out their suggestions one by one, eg *Number five — the,* and you tell them if that is correct or not. They need not guess in order, 1, 2, 3, etc; they can start in the middle if they prefer. For your purposes, it would be helpful to number the words on your copy of the lyric so you can respond quickly to their guesses. To do this game, students must use their knowledge of grammar and word order since there is too much to remember from the song. You can make this into a competitive game by dividing the class into two teams. Give a point for each correct guess. When all the gaps have been filled, play the song again.

4 Pronunciation: You could ask students to scan the lyric to find all the examples of words with the sound /w/. (Answers in order: *was, walking, one, when, away, was, way, way, when, went, wild, was, words, when, we, were, when, we, went, we, walked*) Note that spelling and pronunciation differ: *one* does not have *w* and *saw* does not have /w/. Focus on the weak forms of the auxiliaries *was* and *were*; note how the vowel is weakened to a schwa /ə/. Students should pay attention to this as they sing along to the song.

5 Vocabulary: Ask students to find two expressions of great excitement in the lyric (*took my breath away, heart went wild*).

6 Students sing along to the song. Once they know the song, they could sing to the karaoke version.

7 Extension: You could ask students to rewrite the song, but completely changing the situation. The situation should be an important event in their life and they should try to remember what they were doing when that event happened. For example: *I was playing with the computer one day when the postman brought my exam results …*

Grammar page

1 Exercise A concerns the contrast of past simple and continuous in situations where the longer action is interrupted by the shorter one. After A, students could role-play the mini-dialogues between teacher and pupils.

2 Exercise B is preparation for the Game page activity. The dialogue shows the students what kinds of question they will need to ask to solve the puzzles.

Game page

SMALL GROUPS ACTIVITY

Preparation: Make a copy of the Game page for each student in the class. You may want to cut off the answers at the bottom of the page, or ask students to fold the page back.

1 Give each student a copy of the Game page and ask them to look at picture and caption A. Explain that they must ask you questions as in Grammar page exercise B.

2 Answer students' questions according to the solution given on the Game page. Give short yes/no answers such as *Yes, he was* or *No, he didn't*. If a student's question is potentially difficult to understand due to bad grammar, look confused and ask for a repetition. If the question is not relevant to the story, say *Not important*.

3 When several students seem to have got the solution to the story, ask one of them to explain it carefully to the class.

4 Repeat the process for the other three stories. You could ask a volunteer student to read the solution and answer the questions instead of you.

12 I WAS WALKING — Songsheet

A Look at the pictures and questions. What is this song about? How many questions can you answer already?

1 Where was Henry walking?
2 How did Henry feel?
3 Who did Henry see?
4 How did Henry feel then?
5 What does Henry remember to this day?
6 What happened to Henry's heart?
7 What did Karen do when Henry was trying to think of something to say?
8 What happened when they were standing there?
9 What did they do then?
10 How long did they stay there?

B Listen and answer the questions or check your answers.

C Guess the missing words of the song. Use the questions above, your memory and your knowledge of grammar!

Example: *Number 5 — the!*

```
____  ____  _____ing  ____
 1     2       3          4

the  _____  ____  ____
 5      6       7     8

____  ____  ____  ____
 9    10    11    12
```

Yeah you really took my breath away
Nothing I could do

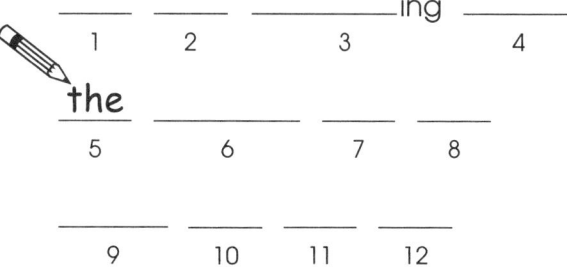

```
____  ____  _____ing  ____
 13    14      15         16

____  ____  ____  ____  ____
 17    18    19    20    21
```

And I remember to this day
The way you looked at me
The way you made me feel

When I saw you on the street that day
My heart went wild

```
____  ____  _____ing  ____  ____
 22    23      24         25    26

____  _____  ____  ____
 27     28      29     30

____  ____  _____ed  ____  _____ed
 31    32      33        34      35

____  ____  _____ing  ____
 36    37      38         39

____  ____  ____  ____  ____
 40    41    42    43    44
```

So we went to a cafe
We walked into that room
And stayed all afternoon

D Listen again to check your answers.

From **Singing Grammar** by Mark Hancock © Cambridge University Press 1998 **PHOTOCOPIABLE** 59

Grammar page

I WAS WALKING 12

A Look at the pictures and write the other children's answers to the teacher's question.

What happened to you?!

Well, you see, I was sitting quietly reading a book when suddenly somebody threw a lot of water over me.

B In this dialogue, the speakers are playing a guessing game. The person asking questions has to discover what happened to the boy in the picture. Read the dialogue and write what happened to Tom. Begin like this: *One afternoon, Tom was ...*

Tom opens his eyes. He sees the school. The car park is empty. He shouts 'Oh, no!' and gets off the bus quickly.

Was Tom going to school?
No, he wasn't.
Was it in the morning?
No, it wasn't.
Was it in the afternoon?
Yes, it was.
Was Tom going home?
Yes, he was.
Did he sleep on the bus?
Yes, he did.
Did he go past the bus stop?
Yes, he did.
Did he wake up when the bus was returning past the school?
Yes, he did.

From **Singing Grammar** by Mark Hancock © Cambridge University Press 1998 **PHOTOCOPIABLE**

---

answers

A Paul: Well, you see, I was running across the playground when somebody put their leg out and I fell and hurt my knees.
Janet: Well, you see, I was walking along and looking at Sue and suddenly I walked into a post and hurt my face.
Lola: Well, you see, I was practising with my basketball when somebody stole it and ran away with it.
Mike: Well, you see, I was lying in the playground sleeping and somebody took my trousers.

B One afternoon, Tom was going home from school. While he was sitting on the bus, he fell asleep. He was sleeping when the bus passed his bus stop. The bus reached the end of its journey and began the return journey. Tom woke up when the bus was passing the school again.

60

12 | I WAS WALKING
Game page

Ask *yes/no* questions to discover what happened to these people.

A

Barney arrives home. There is a bloody cut above his ear. His walkman is broken and he has ice-cream all down his shirt. He has his school bag. A friend is with him. This friend does not normally walk home with Barney because he goes to a different school.

C

Mike is walking along a country road carrying bicycle bags and a cyclist's helmet. In his bag he has a parcel in brightly coloured paper. He has grass in his hair and his face is sunburnt. Suddenly, he finds his bike at the side of the road, bent and broken.

B

Joanna is standing in a telephone box. She is wearing her dressing gown and slippers and her hair is wet. She has a parcel under her arm. On the phone, she can hear her answer machine. She is thinking bad things about her brother's taste in music.

D

Debbie and Jill are walking along the beach. They are carrying artist's equipment. They have painted pictures of a sunset. It is early morning and they are tired and sick from eating too much chocolate.

From **Singing Grammar** by Mark Hancock © Cambridge University Press 1998 **PHOTOCOPIABLE**

---

answers

A Barney was walking home from school eating an ice-cream and listening to his walkman. On the other side of the street, he saw his friend going home from a different school. He turned to look at his friend and walked into a tree. His friend saw his accident and walked home with him.

B Joanna was having a shower when the doorbell rang. She wanted her brother to answer it, but he couldn't hear it because he was listening to loud music. Finally, she went to answer the door. The postman, with a parcel, was just leaving. She walked out to take the parcel and the door closed behind her. Her brother couldn't hear the doorbell, so she decided to telephone him because the telephone was near his room.

C Mike was cycling to a friend's birthday party. He was early and he decided to sleep in a field. While he was sleeping, a thief stole his bike. While the thief was escaping, he was hit by a car. He left the broken bike by the road.

D The girls went to the rock in the evening to paint a picture of the sunset. While they were painting, the sea came in and the rock became an island. They were trapped on the island until the tide went out again in the morning. While they were waiting on the island, they ate a lot of chocolate because they were hungry and there was nothing else to eat.

61

SECTION THREE INTERMEDIATE
13

Grammar
first conditional

Music
ballad + karaoke

Topic
In this song, the singer promises to help a friend if they have problems.

If you're tired and lonely
I'll come to you
If you need someone you can talk to
I'll be there for you

If your friends desert you
I'll be by your side
If you need a place to go
My door is open wide

If you're feeling cold
I'll build a fire
If you're feeling sad and low
I'll take you higher

If you're lonely

Songsheet

1 Prediction: Ask students to fold the Songsheet so they can only see the pictures. Students predict what the song is about.
2 Gist: Play the song. Students note words they hear and check their predictions.
3 Pronunciation: Students unfold the Songsheet and complete the lyric. They could use a phonemic chart from a coursebook or dictionary if they want to use the phonetic clues beneath each gap. Play the song again for them to check their answers.
Note: All of the missing words have in common the letter *r*. However, in all the words except *friends*, it follows a vowel. When an *r* follows a vowel, it is not pronounced in many variants of English (such as that in the song). Note that it <u>is</u> pronounced in *door* because the following word (*is*) begins with a vowel; the /r/ sound serves to separate the vowel sound in *door* from the vowel sound in *is*.
4 Vocabulary: Students scan the lyric for adjectives of feeling. You could discuss if any of them are metaphors. For example, *cold* may be a metaphor, and the response to it *I'll build a fire* almost certainly is.
5 Students could sing along to the song. Once they know the song, they could sing to the karaoke version.
6 Extension: Students could write more verses for the song and sing them to the karaoke version.

Grammar page

1 Exercise A shows that various tenses are possible in conditionals, but not *will* in the *if* clause. In the examples, there are present simple and continuous in the *if* clauses, and imperatives, modals and future simple in the main clauses.
Note: At a more advanced level, students may come across *will* in the *if* clause with the special meaning of insistent habit, eg *If you will keep playing with matches, then of course you'll get burnt.*
2 Exercise B could lead on to further work on the topic of a 'virtual holiday'. Students could think of other attractions to include in an advert.
3 Exercise C highlights the variety of structures possible in the main clause. You could ask students to identify the various functions of the conditionals they write, such as *offering, advising, suggesting, predicting.*
4 Exercise D is preparation for the Game page activity, showing how conditionals can be used to guess at a friend's problems and offer help.

Game page

PAIRS ACTIVITY

Preparation: Make one copy of the page for each pair of students. Cut out the cards or provide scissors for the students to do this.
1 Give out the cards and rule sheets to students in pairs. Ask them to read the rules.
2 You could demonstrate the game with a volunteer. The volunteer takes a card and you ask questions to guess at the problem on the card.
3 Leave students to play the game together.

13 IF YOU'RE LONELY — Songsheet

A You will hear a song related to these pictures.
What do you think the song is about?

B Listen to the song and note down words you hear.

C Complete the song. Get help from the phonetic transcriptions. What do all the missing words have in common? Listen and check.

If _____ _____ and lonely, I'll come to you
　　/jə/　　/taɪəd/

If you need someone you can talk to, I'll be _____ ____ you
　　　　　　　　　　　　　　　　　　　　　　/ðeə/　/fə/

If ____ _____ _____ you, I'll be by your side
　/jə/　/frendz/　/dɪzɜːt/

If you need a place to go, my ____ is open wide
　　　　　　　　　　　　　/dɔː(r)/

If _____ feeling cold, I'll build a ____
　　/jə/　　　　　　　　　　　/faɪə/

If _____ feeling sad and low, I'll take you _____
　　/jə/　　　　　　　　　　　　　　　　　　/haɪə/

From **Singing Grammar** by Mark Hancock © Cambridge University Press 1998　**PHOTOCOPIABLE**

Grammar page

IF YOU'RE LONELY **13**

A Identify the incorrect sentence and underline the correct word in the rule.

If clause	Main clause
1 If you're going out later,	you should take an umbrella.
2 If you'll have any problems,	call us.
3 If you don't pay,	they'll call the police.

Rule: Don't use (*will* / *be* / *do*) in the *if* clause.

B Read this text. What is it about? Where does it come from? If there are any mistakes, correct them.

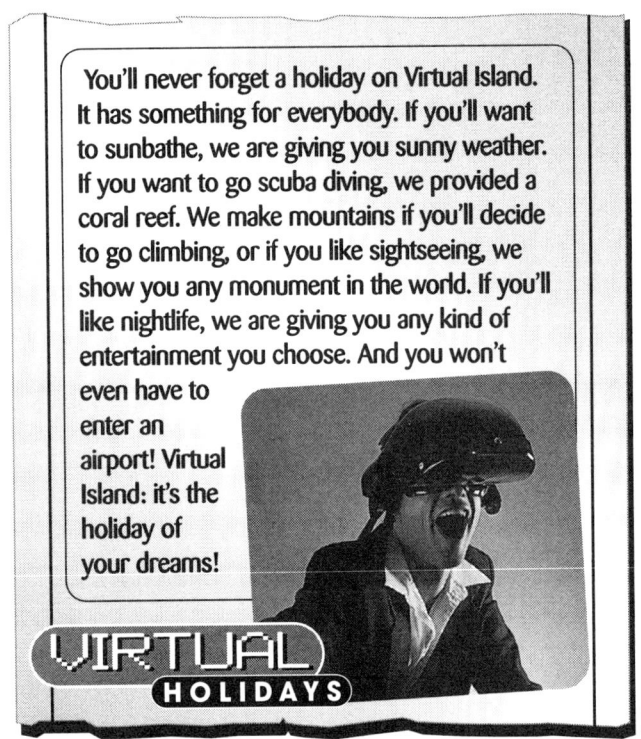

You'll never forget a holiday on Virtual Island. It has something for everybody. If you'll want to sunbathe, we are giving you sunny weather. If you want to go scuba diving, we provided a coral reef. We make mountains if you'll decide to go climbing, or if you like sightseeing, we show you any monument in the world. If you'll like nightlife, we are giving you any kind of entertainment you choose. And you won't even have to enter an airport! Virtual Island: it's the holiday of your dreams!

VIRTUAL HOLIDAYS

C Write *if* clauses for these main clauses.

Example: *If you're late*, he'll be really angry. OR He'll be really angry *if you're late*.

1 you can borrow my camera

2 I'll look after your dog for you

3 you should see a doctor

4 let's go tomorrow instead

5 why don't you tell her?

6 they'll be out of the league

D Complete this dialogue.

— Are you OK, Laura?
— Yeah, OK I suppose.
— Look, if you're worried about the exam tomorrow, _____.
— No, I've studied a lot already.
— Well, if you've got a problem with your boyfriend, _____.
— No, I'm getting on fine with John.
— It's your driving test on Friday, isn't it? If you're worried about it, _____.
— Oh, will you? That's great, thanks!

From **Singing Grammar** by Mark Hancock © Cambridge University Press 1998   **PHOTOCOPIABLE**

---

answers

A Incorrect: 2 (If you have ...)
Rule: Don't use *will* in the *if* clause.

B The text is about holidays, virtual reality. The text is an advertisement from a magazine, a newspaper, a notice board, the internet.
... if you **want** to sunbathe, we'll **give** you sunny weather. If you want to go scuba diving, we'll **provide** a coral reef. We'll **make** mountains if you **decide** to go climbing, or if you like sightseeing, we'll **show** you any monument in the world. If you like nightlife, we'll **give** you any kind of entertainment you choose ...

C Examples:
1 You can borrow my camera if yours is broken.
2 If you're going on holiday, I'll look after your dog for you.
3 If your back still hurts, you should see a doctor.
4 If you're busy today, let's go tomorrow instead.
5 If you love her, why don't you tell her?
6 If they lose this match, they'll be out of the league.

D Examples: I'll study with you; let's talk about it; I'll take you for a practice drive

64

13 IF YOU'RE LONELY — Game page

Rules

1 Play this game with a partner.

2 Your partner takes a card. On the card there is one of these problems:

- exam tomorrow
- split up with girl/boyfriend
- no money
- lonely
- driving test
- bored
- headache
- parents don't understand
- dog died
- no tickets for concert
- team lost the match
- bad school report
- computer broken
- bike stolen
- ????

3 You must guess your partner's problem by offering help or advice. Use conditional clauses.
Examples: *If you need money, I'll lend you some.*
If your computer's broken, I'll look at it for you.

4 If you don't guess the correct problem, your partner should refuse your help.
Example: *No, that's not the problem.*

5 If you guess the problem, your partner should accept your help.
Example: *Oh, that's great! Thanks a lot!*
Then it's your turn to take a card.

You are unhappy because your parents do not understand you. They always shout at you.	You are afraid because your school report is bad and your parents will be very angry.	You are sad because your favourite football team lost a very important match.
You are angry because you left your bike outside a shop and somebody stole it.	You are sad because you had a fight with your boy/girlfriend and you are splitting up.	You are angry because the hard disk broke on your computer and you have lost your best games.
You are unhappy because all your friends are going to a concert but there are no tickets left.	You are nervous because you have a driving test tomorrow.	You are nervous because you have an exam tomorrow and you haven't studied.
You are sad because your dog died. You loved your dog very much.	You have a headache. You have taken some aspirin but the headache will not go away.	You are sad because you can't go out; you can't go out because you haven't got any money.
You are lonely. You moved to this area recently and you don't have any friends.	You are bored. There is nothing to do in the place where you live.	You decide. Write your problem here: _____

From **Singing Grammar** by Mark Hancock © Cambridge University Press 1998 **PHOTOCOPIABLE**

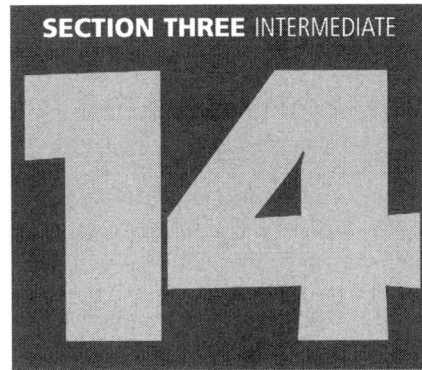

SECTION THREE INTERMEDIATE
14

Grammar
past simple narrative

Music
jazz + karaoke

Topic
This song tells the story of a forbidden romance involving the daughter of an important gangster. The pronouns *she* and *he* are used, and we are not told who these refer to. This technique to provoke curiosity is often used on film advertising posters. More background to the story is provided on the Grammar page.

She came in through the door
Everybody looked
He went across the floor
And stood with her and talked
He asked her for a dance
They danced through the night
Everybody thought
'That dance will be the last dance of
   their lives'

It was a dangerous romance
But they didn't care
From the first time that they danced
It was a life or death affair

Then they left the bar
Everybody saw
They jumped into a car
And as they closed the door
They heard somebody say
'They'll catch you both one day'
But they drove onto the highway
And tried to get away

It was a dangerous …

It was a dangerous romance

It was a dangerous romance

Dangerous romance

Songsheet
1 Prediction: Ask students to say what is happening in the strip cartoon.
2 Gist: Play the song. Students check their predictions. They could note any words they think are important.
3 Detail: Students complete the lyric on the Songsheet and then listen again to check and complete it.
4 Pronunciation: Focus on how the regular verbs in the past tense are pronounced. The past tense ending *-ed* is not pronounced as a separate syllable unless the infinitive of the verb ends in the sounds /d/ or /t/. For example, *walk* and *walked* are both only one syllable. *Walked* ends with the consonant cluster /kt/. These clusters are often difficult for students to pronounce.
5 Students sing along to the song, paying attention to these verbs. Once they know the song, they could sing to the karaoke version.
Note: At the end of the Grammar page, students are asked to write another verse for the song. This could also be sung to the karaoke version.

Grammar page
1 Exercise A concerns regular and irregular past simple verbs in the affirmative and negative, and provides some background to the story in the song.
2 Exercise B focuses on the question form. The beginnings of the questions (*Did they … What did they … Where did they … Who …*) should each be used twice.
3 After writing their own third verses, students could sing them to the karaoke version. Alternatively, the class could pool their ideas and make a third verse all together to sing.
4 Extension: Students could retell or rewrite the story in a different genre. For example, they could write it as a newspaper report. In the song, the pronouns *she* and *he* are used, and we are not told who these refer to. This technique to provoke curiosity is often used on film advertising posters, but not in newspaper journalism; students' news reports should be more explicit.
Alternatively, students could design a film advertising poster for the story and choose famous actors and actresses for the main roles. They could also write a summary of the plot for a magazine's cinema page. Such film summaries are normally written in present tenses.

Game page
INDIVIDUAL / PAIRS ACTIVITY
1 Give out the Game page and explain that it is a maze or labyrinth. Students look at the illustration, which shows how the game works. You could demonstrate by copying the top left hand corner of the puzzle on the board and going through the first few moves together with the whole class.
2 Students find a path through the maze alone or in pairs.
3 Go through the answers with the class, asking them to repeat the words on the route with the right number of syllables. The correct route is:
kill — look — dance — walk — help — plan — stop — close — talk — climb — ask — vote — add — hate — wait — end — start — taste — want — need — catch — come — drive — see — get — stand — go — hear — think — leave — wake — ring — swim — drink — eat

66

14 DANGEROUS ROMANCE — Songsheet

A Explain what is happening in this story.

She _____ _____ through the door, everybody _____

He _____ across the floor, and _____ _____ _____ _____

He _____ _____ for a dance, _____ _____ through the night.

Everybody _____, 'That dance will be the last dance of their lives'

Then they _____ _____ _____, everybody _____

They jumped _____ _____ _____ and as they _____ _____ _____ _____

They _____ somebody say, 'They'll catch you both one day'

But they _____ onto the highway, and _____ to get away

It was a dangerous romance
But they didn't care
From the first time that they danced
It was a life or death affair

B Listen and check your predictions.

C Complete the lyric of the song. Then listen to check your answers.

From **Singing Grammar** by Mark Hancock © Cambridge University Press 1998 — PHOTOCOPIABLE

Grammar page — DANGEROUS ROMANCE 14

A Why was the romance dangerous? Complete this text to find the reason. Use the correct forms of these verbs:

work go control tell meet discover
say hate fall want think like

Chicago, 1930: Two Mafia chiefs (1) _____ the city. Their names were Tony Tyrone and Al Mantini. Tony (2) _____ Al, and Al didn't (3) _____ Tony. They (4) _____ to kill each other. Tony had a daughter called Annie. One evening, Annie (5) _____ Jim. Jim (6) _____ for Al Mantini; he was the manager of one of Al's bars. They (7) _____ in love. Tyrone (8) _____ this and he was very angry. He (9) _____ Annie not to see Jim again, 'Or I'll kill you both!' Annie didn't (10) _____ anything, but she (11) _____, 'You control half of Chicago, but you don't control me!' Later that evening, she (12) _____ to Jim's bar ...

B What happened next? Make eight questions from these words and phrases:

Did they ...   get away?   What did they ...
Where did they ...   do to earn money?
do when Tyrone's men arrived?   drive to?
followed them?   return to Chicago?
helped them?   decide to live?   Who ...

Invent answers to your questions or choose them from these speech bubbles:

C Can you continue the story of Annie and Jim? Write your story as another verse for the song. Try to put rhyming words at the end of the lines, to match the first two verses.

From **Singing Grammar** by Mark Hancock © Cambridge University Press 1998   **PHOTOCOPIABLE**

---

answers

A 1 controlled 2 hated 3 like 4 wanted 5 met 6 worked 7 fell 8 discovered 9 told 10 say 11 thought 12 went

B Did they: return to Chicago/get away? What did they: do when Tyrone's men arrived/do to earn money? Where did they: decide to live/drive to? Who: followed them/helped them?

C A possible third verse:
They drove out of Chicago, they drove right through the day
Did the gunmen catch them, or did they get away?
What did they do at the end of the road? Where did they go then?
The only thing I know is, we never saw them again

68

14 DANGEROUS ROMANCE

Game page

Rules

1 Play individually or in pairs.

2 Find your way through this maze.

3 Move from square to square horizontally or vertically like this: ⟶

4 You can only cross squares if *

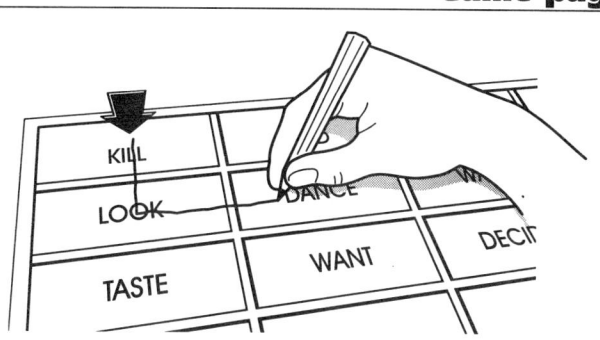

* the past tense has one syllable

KILL	NEED	HELP	PLAN	STOP	HATE
LOOK	DANCE	WALK	END	CLOSE	VISIT
TASTE	WANT	DECIDE	WAIT	TALK	CLIMB
NOTE	ENTER	FINISH	ARRIVE	ADD	ASK

* the past tense has two syllables

HELP	DANCE	WALK	PHONE	JUMP	VOTE
TASTE	START	END	WAIT	HATE	ADD
WANT	PLAN	STOP	CLOSE	TALK	LOOK
NEED	CLIMB	ASK	RAIN	ARRIVE	KILL

* the past tense is irregular

CATCH	COME	STOP	LEAVE	WAKE	RING
DANCE	DRIVE	LOOK	THINK	WALK	SWIM
WAIT	SEE	TALK	HEAR	ENTER	DRINK
HELP	GET	STAND	GO	WANT	EAT

From **Singing Grammar** by Mark Hancock © Cambridge University Press 1998 **PHOTOCOPIABLE**

SECTION THREE INTERMEDIATE

Grammar
present perfect for experiences

Music
latin pop + karaoke

Topic
In the first part of the song, the singer tells the story of a secret passion for a girl called Josephine. His words are addressed to Josephine; they may be what he really says to her when they meet, or they may just be in his head. He uses the present perfect to talk about his experiences.
In the third verse, the singer addresses us, the listeners, to report the unhappy outcome of his meeting with Josephine last night. In this part of the song, he is referring to a specific past time, so he switches from the present perfect to past simple tense.

I know you've never seen my face
You've never heard my name
Although I've never talked to you
I've got you on the brain

Josephine, I've seen you in my dreams
Josephine, I've seen you in my dreams

I've never had the confidence
To talk to you before
The time has come and here I am
Knocking on your door

Josephine ...

I talked to Josephine last night
And now she knows my name
I told her how I feel and then
She looked at me as if I was insane
Josephine
You know I've never felt so stupid before
Standing at Josephine's door
You know I've never felt so stupid before
Standing at Josephine's door

Josephine ...

Josephine

Songsheet

1 Prediction: Ask students to fold the Songsheet so they can't see the lyric exercise. Students list the verbs under the pictures. There is no fixed answer: if one person thinks *feel* should go under *eye*, it is not a problem.
2 Detail: Play the song. Students tick the verbs from the prediction exercise that they hear in the song.
3 Students unfold the Songsheet and play this text completion game: they call out their suggestions one by one, eg *Number five — seen*, and you tell them if that is correct or not. They need not guess in order, 1, 2, 3, etc; they can start in the middle if they prefer. For your purposes, it would be helpful to number the words on your copy of the lyric so you can respond quickly to their guesses. To do this game, students must use their knowledge of grammar and word order since there is too much to remember from the song. You can make this into a competitive game by dividing the class into two teams. Give a point for each correct guess. Students may want clues to help them and may ask for explanations of the grammatical labels, which are as follows:
pro = pronoun, *aux* = auxiliary verb, *p.part* = past participle, *prep* = preposition, *art* = article, *conj* = conjunction, *poss* = possessive adjective, *pres.part* = present participle
When all the gaps have been filled, play the song again.
4 Pronunciation: Focus attention on the pronunciation of the contractions *I've* and *you've*.
5 Students sing along to the song. Once they know the song, they could sing to the karaoke version.
6 Extension: You could ask students to write out the dialogue between Josephine and the singer when they talk at her front door. Students could discuss their own embarrassing experiences.

Grammar page

1 Exercises A, B and C focus on statements and questions about experiences. Students should work in pairs in exercise C to ask and answer their questions.
2 Exercise D focuses on the switch from present perfect to past simple when the conversation moves into more specific detail about an experience. This exercise is preparation for the Game page activity.

Game page

PAIRS ACTIVITY
1 Give out the Game page and ask students to read the rules.
2 You could demonstrate by making your own line. Include a few lies. Students then ask you questions to discover where your line is. Once they have found your line, ask them if they think you have told any lies.
3 Leave students in pairs to draw their lines and play the game. Remind them to switch to past simple if they want to ask for more details (rule 5). Point out that they will need to change the verbs in the boxes into past participles.

15 JOSEPHINE **Songsheet**

A Put these verbs under the pictures:
hear cry feel talk look dream listen tell watch speak think see know sing

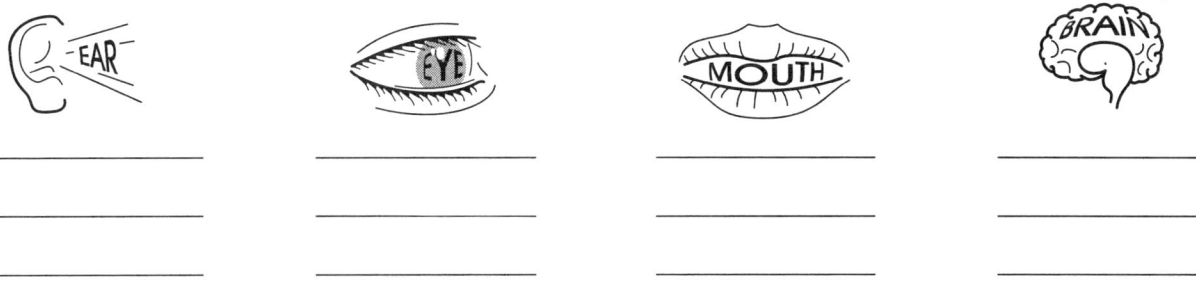

B Listen to the song and tick (✓) the verbs you hear.

C Guess the missing words of the song. Use your memory and your knowledge of parts of speech!
Example: *Number 5 — seen!*

___ ___ ___ ___ **seen** ___ ___
pro verb pro/aux adverb p.part poss noun
 1   2   3   4   5   6   7

___ ___ ___ ___ ___ , ___ ___ ___
pro/aux adverb p.part poss noun   conj pro/aux adverb
   8   9   10   11   12   13   14   15

___ ___ ___ ___ ___ ___ ___ ___ ___
p.part prep pro pro/aux p.part pro prep art noun
  16   17   18   19   20   21   22   23   24

Josephine, I've seen you in my dreams **(repeat)**

___ ___ ___ ___ ___ ___ ___ ___ ___
pro/aux adverb p.part art abstract noun prep infinitive prep pro
  25   26   27   28   29   30   31   32   33

___ , ___ ___ ___ ___ ___ ___ ___ ___
adverb   art noun aux p.part conj adverb pro aux
  34   35   36   37   38   39   40   41   42

___ ___ ___ ___
pres.part prep poss noun
   43   44   45   46

Josephine ...

I talked to Josephine last night
And now she knows my name
I told her how I feel and then
She looked at me as if I was insane
Josephine
You know I've never felt so stupid ⎫
  before   ⎬ repeat
Standing at Josephine's door   ⎭

Josephine ...

D Listen again to check your answers.

From **Singing Grammar** by Mark Hancock © Cambridge University Press 1998 **PHOTOCOPIABLE** 71

Grammar page

JOSEPHINE **15**

A Look at Joanne's photos. Write things you think she's done.

Example: *She's met a rock star.*

B Make ten true sentences about yourself from these words and phrases:

I've	felt	during a sad film	seen
in love	cried	an English breakfast
a football match	eaten	to London
to a famous person	been	dreamt
in the shower	a famous picture
in public	heard	to a police officer
about flying	never	karaoke
a kung fu film	drunk	watched
stupid	Indian food	seasick
Irish music	talked	sung

C Make your sentences into questions with *ever* and ask a partner.

Example: *Have you ever cried during a sad film?*

D Look at this interview and put the verbs in the correct tense.

A: (1) _____ (you make) a snowman?

B: Yes, I have.

A: OK. And (2) _____ (you see) a shark?

B: Yes, I have.

A: Oh, really? Where (3) _____ (you see) it?

B: In Australia.

A: Wow! You (4) _____ (go) to Australia!

B: Yes, I have. We (5) _____ (go) there last winter. It was great.

From **Singing Grammar** by Mark Hancock © Cambridge University Press 1998 **PHOTOCOPIABLE**

---

answers

A She's won a tennis competition/championship. She's been on a plane. She's been to Paris. She's broken a leg. She's ridden a horse. She's climbed a mountain. She's played the piano in a concert.

B Examples: I've felt stupid. I've eaten an English breakfast. I've never talked to a famous person ...

C Examples: Have you ever felt stupid? Have you ever eaten an English breakfast? Have you ever talked to a famous person? ...

D 1 Have you (ever) made 2 have you (ever) seen 3 did you see 4 've been 5 went

72

15 JOSEPHINE

Game page

Rules

1. Play this game in pairs.

2. Have you ever done any of the things in the squares? Tick (✓) the things you have done.

3. Can you make a complete path from side to side or top to bottom like this? ⟶
Diagonal lines are not allowed. If *no*, lie; say you have done some things to complete the path.

4. Work with a partner. Ask questions as in exercise C on the Grammar page. Find your partner's path.

5. If you think your partner is lying, challenge your partner to give more details.
Example: *Oh really? You've seen a shark? Where did you see it?*

6. Take turns to ask questions. The first to find their partner's path wins.

7. After the game, check your suspicions. Ask your partner which were the lies.

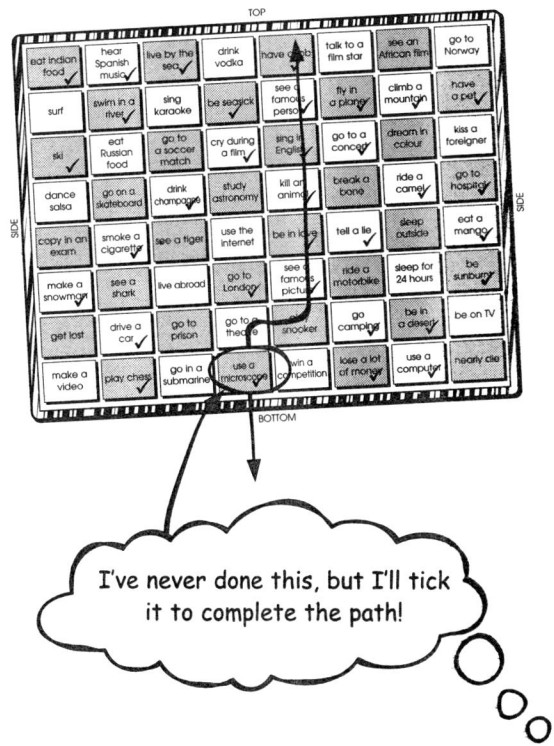

I've never done this, but I'll tick it to complete the path!

TOP

eat Indian food	hear Spanish music	live by the sea	drink vodka	have a job	talk to a film star	see an African film	go to Norway
surf	swim in a river	sing karaoke	be seasick	see a famous person	fly in a plane	climb a mountain	have a pet
ski	eat Russian food	go to a soccer match	cry during a film	sing in English	go to a concert	dream in colour	kiss a foreigner
dance salsa	go on a skateboard	drink champagne	study astronomy	kill an animal	break a bone	ride a camel	go to hospital
copy in an exam	smoke a cigarette	see a tiger	use the internet	be in love	tell a lie	sleep outside	eat a mango
make a snowman	see a shark	live abroad	go to London	see a famous picture	ride a motorbike	sleep for 24 hours	be sunburnt
get lost	drive a car	go to prison	go to a theatre	play snooker	go camping	be in a desert	be on TV
make a video	play chess	go in a submarine	use a microscope	win a competition	lose a lot of money	use a computer	nearly die

BOTTOM

From **Singing Grammar** by Mark Hancock © Cambridge University Press 1998 **PHOTOCOPIABLE** 73

SECTION THREE INTERMEDIATE — 16

Grammar
used to for past habits and states

Music
ballad + karaoke

Topic
The singer tells us how a boy pretended to love her in order to meet her best friend. Now she is no longer in love with the boy and is not friends with the girl.

I used to love a boy
And I used to think he loved me
Now I know that I was wrong

He left me for a girl
Who used to be my friend
Now I know he loved her all along

But he used to say sweet things to me
And I always used to believe him
He used to say sweet things to me
(repeat)

He used me to be near her
Pretending that he loved me
All the things he used to say were lies

Then one day I watched them
Dancing in each other's arms
That was when I realized

But he ...

Sweet things

Songsheet

Preparation: Make one copy of the Songsheet page for every two students in the class and cut it into Songsheets A and B. Give out the Songsheets so that students with Songsheet A can sit near a partner with Songsheet B.

1 Prediction: Ask students to fold the Songsheet so they cannot see the words and describe their pictures to their partners to discover the difference. Then explain that they will hear a song about one of the pictures. Ask them to predict (in general terms) what the song is about.

2 Gist: Play the song. Students must decide which of the two pictures shows the situation in the song. (Answer: *the picture on Songsheet A*)

3 Information gap: Students unfold the Songsheet and work with a partner who has the other version of the Songsheet. Ask them to find differences between the lyrics on their Songsheets without looking at their partner's sheet.

Note: In all cases, the difference is whether the line has *used to* or not. In all cases, both versions would be grammatically correct.

4 Detail: Play the song and ask students to note which lines are correct on their Songsheet and which are correct on their partner's Songsheet. They should then correct their Songsheet so it contains the words of the song.

5 Pronunciation: Focus on the pronunciation of the *s* in *used*: it is an /s/ in *used to* but a /z/ when *used* means *utilize*, eg *He used me to be near her*. Also, you could ask students to listen to the pronunciation of the weak forms *to*, *was*, *a* and *I*.

6 Students sing along to the song. Once they know the song, they could sing to the karaoke version.

7 Extension: Students could imagine they are the ex-friend or the ex-boyfriend from the song and tell the story from that point of view. This could be done in the form of a diary entry or a conversation with the *me* of the song. Note that the emphasis would probably be different from these points of view as the characters try to justify their actions.

Grammar page

1 Exercise A focuses on distinguishing *used to* (past habit or state) from *used* (meaning *utilize*).

2 In exercise B, students write sentences using *used to* to describe past habits or states.

3 Exercise C asks students to identify situations where *used to* is not used, that is single events in the past. This exercise leads to the Game page activity.

Game page

INDIVIDUAL / PAIRS ACTIVITY

1 Give out the Game page and explain that it is a maze or labyrinth. You could go through the first few moves as a whole class to get them started.

2 Students find a path through the maze alone or in pairs.

3 Go through the answers with the class. The correct route is:
wear glasses — have long hair — live in the country — be a vegetarian —
play football at weekends — like ice-cream — walk to school — collect stamps —
have piano lessons — hate school — play with dolls — have a goldfish —
get toys for Christmas — play with model cars — paint pictures —
hate tomatoes — drink a lot of lemonade — fight with my brother

16 SWEET THINGS **Songsheet**

Songsheet A

A Find a partner with Songsheet B. Describe your pictures and find the difference without looking at your partner's sheet.

B Listen to the song. Is it about your picture or your partner's picture?

C Find differences between your lyrics without looking at your partner's Songsheet. Note down the differences.
Example: A: *My first line is 'I loved a boy'.*
B: *OK, that's different. My first line is 'I used to love a boy'.*

I loved a boy
And I used to think he loved me
Now I know that I was wrong

He left me for a girl
Who used to be my friend
Now I know he used to love her all along

But he said sweet things to me
And I always used to believe him
He said sweet things to me

He used to use me to be near her
Pretending that he loved me
All the things he used to say were lies

Then one day I watched them
Dancing in each other's arms
That was when I realized

D Listen to the song. Which of your lines were correct? Which of your partner's lines were correct? Correct your lyric.

Songsheet B

A Find a partner with Songsheet A. Describe your pictures and find the difference without looking at your partner's sheet.

B Listen to the song. Is it about your picture or your partner's picture?

C Find differences between your lyrics without looking at your partner's Songsheet. Note down the differences.
Example: B: *My first line is 'I used to love a boy'.*
A: *OK, that's different. My first line is 'I loved a boy'.*

I used to love a boy
And I thought he loved me
Now I know that I was wrong

He left me for a girl
Who was my friend
Now I know he loved her all along

But he used to say sweet things to me
And I always believed him
He used to say sweet things to me

He used me to be near her
Pretending that he used to love me
All the things he said were lies

Then one day I watched them
Dancing in each other's arms
That was when I realized

D Listen to the song. Which of your lines were correct? Which of your partner's lines were correct? Correct your lyric.

From **Singing Grammar** by Mark Hancock © Cambridge University Press 1998 **PHOTOCOPIABLE** 75

Grammar page

SWEET THINGS 16

A Does the word *used* have an /s/ (<u>s</u>ee) or a /z/ (<u>z</u>oo)?

1 He used me to be near her.
2 She used to be my friend.
3 The car used too much petrol.
4 This building used to be a school.
5 I used to play the piano.
6 We used two hundred pieces of paper.

B Look at the pictures of Oscar ten years ago and Oscar now. Write about him ten years ago, using *used to*.
Example: *He used to wear jeans and a T-shirt.*

Oscar ten years ago

C Which of these sentences could have *used to* instead of the past simple?

1 I lived in a house with a big garden.
2 The neighbours often had parties.
3 I started at this school last year.
4 We moved to Rome three years ago.
5 I got this guitar for my birthday.
6 I didn't eat vegetables when I was a child.
7 My older sister bullied me.
8 I learnt to ride a bike when I was six.
9 I was born in 1979.
10 I wore glasses but now I wear contact lenses.
11 My father drew this picture.
12 I was in the school play last year.

Oscar now

From **Singing Grammar** by Mark Hancock © Cambridge University Press 1998 **PHOTOCOPIABLE**

---

answers

A /s/ = 2, 4, 5   /z/ = 1, 3, 6

B Examples: He used to read *The World*. He used to listen to rock music. He used to have a cat. He used to have a beard. He used to have a lot of hair. He didn't use to wear a tie. He used to be thin. He used to draw pictures. He didn't use to do crosswords.

C Possible with *used to*: 1, 2, 6, 7, 10

76

16 SWEET THINGS

Game page

Rules

1 Play individually or in pairs.

2 Find your way through this maze.

3 Move from square to square horizontally or vertically like this: ⟶

4 You can only go through squares if you can start the sentence in them with *I used to ...*

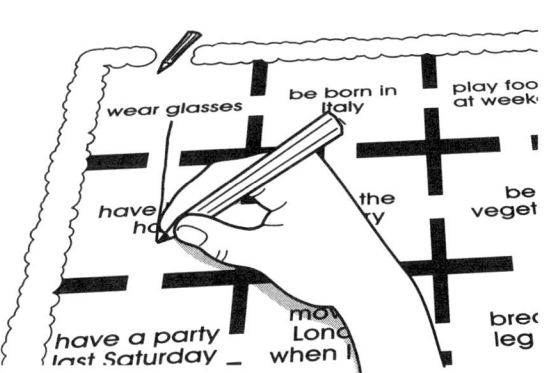

wear glasses	be born in Italy	play football at weekends	like ice-cream	walk to school
have long hair	live in the country	be a vegetarian	start school when I was five	collect stamps
have a party last Saturday	move to London when I was twelve	break my leg once	hate school	have piano lessons
get this bike for my birthday	get toys for Christmas	have a goldfish	play with dolls	start learning the piano last year
make this model car	play with model cars	buy a goldfish last weekend	buy this doll	write this poem
paint this picture	paint pictures	hate tomatoes	drink a lot of lemonade	fight with my brother

From **Singing Grammar** by Mark Hancock © Cambridge University Press 1998 **PHOTOCOPIABLE**

SECTION THREE INTERMEDIATE

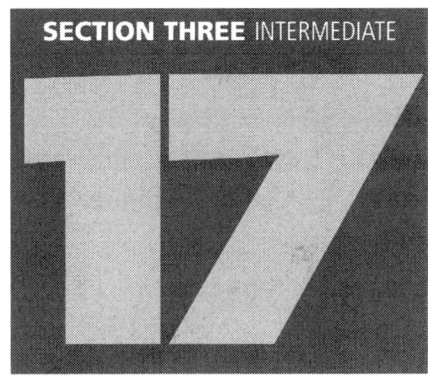

Grammar
past perfect

Music
rock + karaoke

Topic
The singer, a teenage boy, narrates three short episodes which result in him getting into trouble.

I was sitting in the bedroom playing my guitar one evening
Then I remembered I'd started making toast
So I rushed downstairs and I ran into the kitchen
But the toast had burnt and the house was full of smoke
My mother said, 'Son, look what you've done!'
I said, 'Oh no, I'm in trouble again!'

Saturday night I decided to invite some friends round
My parents had gone out, I was home alone
We put the music on loud and we used the house like a playground
We'd made an awful mess when my friends went home
My mother said ...

Sitting on the bus, I noticed I'd forgotten my schoolbag
So I went back home and found I'd forgotten my key, yeah
My mother was out so I climbed in through the window
But I slipped and fell on top of the new TV
My mother said ...
My mother said ...

In trouble again

Songsheet

1 Prediction: Ask students to fold the Songsheet so they can only see the pictures. Explain that there are three episodes represented in the pictures. Students suggest what is happening in each picture.

2 Detail: Play the song. Students order the pictures. (Answers: *1E, 2B, 3A, 4D, 5C*)

3 Students unfold the Songsheet and complete the lyric, using the phonetic transcriptions if that helps them. Play the song again for them to check their answers.

4 Students analyse the lyric to find the chronological order of the events in each verse. (Answers: *1 start making toast/play guitar/toast burn/rush downstairs 2 parents go out/invite friends/put music on and use house like playground/make mess/friends go home 3 forget schoolbag and key/realize forgotten schoolbag/go home/realize forgotten key/climb through window/fall on new TV*)

5 Pronunciation: Focus on the pronunciation of the contractions *I'd* and *we'd* and the weak forms such as *was*, *the*, *a* and *of*.

6 Students sing along to the song.

7 Extension: Students could write more misadventures as verses for the song. They could sing their verses to the karaoke version.

Grammar page

1 You could ask a pair of students to perform the courtroom dialogue in exercise A. The exercise is a puzzle to focus on the 'past in the past' meaning of the past perfect tense. Exercise B asks students to create their own versions of the puzzle. They should use two clauses (one in the past perfect) joined by *when*, *before* or *after*.

2 Exercise C gives practice in forming the past perfect and illustrates a common use of the tense (following verbs such as *realize* when in the past simple).

3 Exercise D is preparation for the Game page activity. Students can use sentences similar to those in exercise C to make their excuses.

Game page

SMALL GROUPS ACTIVITY

Preparation: Make one copy of the Game page for every four students in the class. Cut the page into four as indicated.

1 Divide the class into groups of four. Give each member of the group one of the four different cards on the Game page.

2 Each student completes sentence 1 on their sheet. Then they fold the paper so their sentence cannot be seen.

3 Students pass their paper to the next person in their group. Then each of them completes sentence 2, folds the paper and passes it on. Sentence 2 should contain an example of the past perfect tense.

4 Students continue this process until all four sentences are complete. Then they gather the four papers and put them in a pile in the middle.

5 Students each take a paper and read out the situation and excuse on it. Many of the stories will probably sound bizarre and funny. They could choose their funniest story to role-play in front of the rest of the class.

17 IN TROUBLE AGAIN — Songsheet

A Look at the pictures. How does this boy get into trouble?

B Listen to the song and order the pictures.

C Complete the song. Get help from the phonetic transcriptions. Then listen to check.

____ ____ _____ in the
    /æwəzˑsɪtɪŋ/
bedroom playing my guitar one evening
Then I remembered
____ _____ making toast
  /ædˑstɑːtɪd/
So I rushed downstairs and I ____ into
                    /ræn/
the kitchen
But the _____ ____ _____ and
    /təustədˑbɜːnt/
the house was full of smoke
My mother said, 'Son, look what you've done!'
I said, 'Oh no, I'm in trouble again!'

Saturday night ____ _____ to
               /ædɪˑsaɪdɪd/
invite some friends round
My _____ ____ _____ out, I
    /ˑpeərəntsədˑgɒn/
was home alone

____ ____ the music on loud and
/wɪpʊt/
____ ____ the house like a playground
/wɪjuːzd/
_____ _____ an awful mess when
   /wɪdmeɪd/
my friends went home
My mother said …

Sitting on the bus, I noticed
____ _____ my schoolbag
   /ædfəˑgɒtn/
So ____ _____ back home and
    /æwent/
found ____ _____ my key
       /ædfəˑgɒtn/
My mother was out so ____ _____
                      /æˑklaɪmd/
in through the window
But I slipped ____ _____ on top of
                /ənˑfel/
the new TV

My mother said … **(repeat)**

From **Singing Grammar** by Mark Hancock © Cambridge University Press 1998

Grammar page

IN TROUBLE AGAIN **17**

A Look at this dialogue. Where do you think A and B are? Who are A and B? B did five things; what were they? What order did she do them in?

A: Now, Ms McDonald, just a few more questions. When you had coffee, had you already read the paper?
B: Yes, that's right.
A: And when you read the paper, had you already written a letter?
B: No, I hadn't.
A: I see. So you hadn't written the letter before you read the paper. And had you taken the dog for a walk?
B: Yes, I had.
A: And what did you do after you'd taken the dog for a walk?
B: I went to the cinema.
A: You went to the cinema. One last question, Ms McDonald. What did you do after you'd had coffee?
B: I wrote a letter.
A: Thank you, that will be all.

Order: 1 _____
2 _____
3 _____
4 _____
5 _____

B Write the five actions in exercise A in a different order. Then work with a partner. Imagine you are a lawyer and ask questions to find your partner's order.

C Write a pair of sentences for each picture to describe the situation. Use some of these verbs:

realize   notice   remember   find

Example: 1 *I got out of the car and closed the door. Then I realized that I'd left the key inside.*

D Look at the picture. Who are these people? What has happened? Complete the boy's excuse.

Well, you see, I left the house and went to the bus stop. Then ...

From **Singing Grammar** by Mark Hancock © Cambridge University Press 1998   **PHOTOCOPIABLE**

---

answers

A They are in a courtroom. A is a lawyer and B is a witness.
Order of events: 1 take the dog for a walk 2 go to the cinema 3 read the paper 4 have coffee 5 write a letter

C Examples:
2 I got dressed, had breakfast and went to work. Then I noticed that I'd put on different socks.
3 I went to the postbox and posted the letter. Then I remembered that I hadn't written the address on the letter.
4 I went to the cash machine and put my card in. Then I found I'd forgotten my number.

D They are a student and a teacher. The student has arrived late. Example excuses: Then I realized I hadn't got any money for the bus fare. I noticed I'd forgotten my schoolbag. I realized I'd left my bedroom window open. I noticed I hadn't brought my maths homework.

80

17 IN TROUBLE AGAIN **Game page**

Why I am in trouble with the headteacher

1 Well, I was _____ing _____
_____
_____

2 Then I remembered that _____
_____
_____

3 So I _____
_____
_____

4 but _____
_____

Why the window is broken

1 I was _____ing _____
_____
_____

2 Then I noticed that _____
_____
_____

3 So _____
_____
_____

4 but _____
_____

Why there is food all over my clothes

1 I was _____ing _____
_____
_____

2 Then I realized that _____
_____
_____

3 So _____
_____
_____

4 but _____
_____

Why I haven't done my homework

1 I was _____ing _____
_____
_____

2 Then I found that _____
_____
_____

3 So anyway, I _____
_____
_____

4 So in the end _____
_____

From **Singing Grammar** by Mark Hancock © Cambridge University Press 1998 **PHOTOCOPIABLE**

SECTION THREE INTERMEDIATE

Grammar
present perfect simple/continuous

Music
country + slow version

Topic
This song could be the thoughts of the singer as he waits for his girlfriend to show up for their date. The first verse is after an hour of waiting. The chorus gives some of the background of their new relationship. The last verse is after two hours of waiting.

I've been waiting for an hour
And she's not here yet
Maybe she's stood me up
It's been raining all the time and my
  hair is wet
Now I feel fed up

I've been seeing her for over two
  weeks now
I thought she was mine, all mine
We've been going out dancing almost
  every night
I thought everything was fine

I've been waiting for two hours
Standing here alone
I've been trying to call her on the
  phone
I've been cursing, I've been screaming
'Cause for two weeks I've been
  dreaming
Now the only thing to do is go back
  home

I've been seeing her ...

I've been waiting

Songsheet

Preparation: Make one copy of the Songsheet for each student. Alternatively, make one copy for each pair of students and cut the lines of the jumbled lyric into strips of paper for the students to put in order.

1 Prediction: Ask students to fold the Songsheet (if you haven't cut the lyric into strips) so they can only see the pictures. Ask them to say what might be happening in the pictures and make a list of words they think they might hear in the song.
2 ▭ **Detail:** Play the song. Students tick the words in their list that they hear.
3 Students unfold the Songsheet (alternatively, give out the strips of paper containing the lyric) and find rhyming lines in the lyric. (Answers: *yet/wet, up/up, mine/fine, alone/phone/home, screaming/dreaming*)
4 ▭ Students listen and sequence the lines of the song. Play the song again for students to check.
5 Vocabulary: You could check students know the meaning of *see* in the continuous tense (= *go out with*). You could also check students know the expressions with *up*: *fed up* and *stand up*. You could introduce other phrasal verbs with *up* related to the theme of this song, for example: *show up, turn up, break up, split up, chat up, give up*.
6 Pronunciation: Focus on the links between words with a final vowel sound and following words beginning with a vowel sound. Often, a consonant intrudes to separate the vowels, for example: *for an* (intrusive /r/), *me up* (intrusive /j/), *do is* (intrusive /w/). The rest of the examples in the song are: *hour and* (/r/), *hair is* (/r/), *now I* (/w/), *for over* (/r/), *two hours* (/w/), *here alone* (/r/), *her on* (/r/), *the only* (/j/).
7 ▭ Students sing along to the song. They may find this song difficult to sing at full speed. There is a slow version provided for them to practise with before singing at full speed.
8 Extension: You could ask students to imagine that there has been a mistake and the girl in the song has been waiting for two hours on a different corner. As the boy and girl give up and start going home, they meet each other. Students could script the dialogue between them when they meet.

Grammar page

1 Exercise A focuses on contexts where we can see what people have been doing from the way they look.
Note: In each case, although the simple tense would be correct, the continuous tense gives a more natural emphasis; the writer can see the activities that these people have been doing, but he cannot necessarily say they have finished doing the activities (which is what the present perfect simple would imply).
2 Exercise B looks at the differences between present perfect simple and continuous. Students are asked to complete rules by looking at the examples.
3 Exercise C asks students to apply the rules from B, and it is preparation for the Game page activity.

Game page

SMALL GROUPS ACTIVITY
Preparation: Make one copy of the Game page for every group of two, three or four students in the class. You may want to cut off the answers at the bottom of the page and give them to the groups as a separate strip which they would keep face down on the table. Each group will need a coin, and each player will need a small object to represent themselves, like a counter. You could provide these things or ask students to use something of their own.
1 The rules are on the board, but students should decide what the penalty is for making a grammar mistake in this game. Competitive students could suggest missing a turn. Other students may prefer to help each other on questions of grammar during the game.
2 To demonstrate the game, throw a coin and ask which square you could move to next. For example, if you throw heads, you could move from start to square 1. If you then throw heads again, you could move from square 1 to square 3 and up the ladder to square 6. If you land on the head of a snake, go down the snake to the square below.

18 I'VE BEEN WAITING — Songsheet

A Look at the these pictures. What do you think the song is about?

B Listen and check your predictions.

C Look at the lines from the lyric. Do any of the final words rhyme with final words in another line?

D Listen and put the lines in order. Then listen to check.

- [ ] We've been going out dancing almost every night
- [ ] I've been cursing, I've been screaming
- [ ] Maybe she's stood me up
- [ ] I've been waiting for two hours Standing here alone
- [ ] It's been raining all the time and my hair is wet
- [ ] I thought she was mine, all mine
- [ ] Now the only thing to do is go back home
- [ ] I've been seeing her for over two weeks now
- [ ] I thought everything was fine
- [ ] I've been waiting for an hour And she's not here yet
- [ ] I've been trying to call her on the phone
- [ ] 'Cause for two weeks I've been dreaming
- [ ] Now I feel fed up

From **Singing Grammar** by Mark Hancock © Cambridge University Press 1998

Grammar page

I'VE BEEN WAITING **18**

A What have these people been doing? Complete the letter with a sentence about each one like the example.

Dear Julie,

We've been having a wonderful holiday here in Sunshine Holiday Village. There is so much to do! Today, for example, Alison has been playing tennis. She says she won three matches! (1) _____ in the village swimming pool. (2) _____ in the games room and now his eyes are really red. (3) _____ and she has invited everyone to a fish barbecue tonight. (4) _____ and she looks very sick. I don't think she'll go to the barbecue! (5) _____. He is the only one who does any work here! Unfortunately, I've got flu now and I've been lying in bed all day. What a wonderful holiday! I hope your holiday has been better than mine!

Love from
Sam

B Look at these pairs of sentences, and complete the rules with *simple* or *continuous*.

1 *I've been seeing her for over two weeks now.*
I've seen her three times this week.
Use present perfect _____ to say how many times something happens. Use present perfect _____ to say how long the action continues.

2 *It's rained most of the day, but it's stopped now.*
It's been raining all the time and my hair is wet.
Use present perfect _____ when the action has caused something now. Use present perfect _____ to show that the action is finished.

C Choose the best tense in these sentences:

1 He is a famous footballer. He has _____ (play) for the national team a few times.

2 He doesn't normally smoke, but today he has _____ (smoke) twenty cigarettes.

3 How long have you _____ (learn) French?

4 She's tired because she's _____ (climb) mountains all day.

5 How often have you _____ (watch) a live basketball match?

6 He's _____ (mend) his bicycle and his clothes are covered with oil.

From **Singing Grammar** by Mark Hancock © Cambridge University Press 1998 **PHOTOCOPIABLE**

A 1 John has been swimming 2 Osman has been playing computer games 3 Clara has been fishing 4 Jo has been eating ice-cream 5 Max has been washing up

B 1 simple; continuous 2 continuous; simple

C 1 played 2 smoked 3 been learning 4 been climbing 5 watched 6 been mending

18 I'VE BEEN WAITING — Game page

Rules

1 Play in groups of two, three or four. You need one board and a coin, and a counter for each player.

2 Take turns to throw the coin and move.

3 There are sentences in the squares. Some are best in present perfect simple tense, others are best in present perfect continuous. If the coin shows *Tails*, move to the next present perfect simple square. If the coin shows *Heads*, move to the next present perfect continuous square.

4 If you land on a square with a ladder, go up it. If you land on a square with a snake, go down it. If you land on a square with *Miss your turn*, miss your next turn.

5 The first to **Finish** is the winner.

HEADS = Pres Perf Continuous

TAILS = Pres Perf Simple

20 I've (read) two books since we arrived.	21 It's (rain) for an hour.	22 How many times have you (come) here on holiday?	23 I've (read) all day and my eyes are tired.	FINISH
19 It's (rain) twice this week. **MISS YOUR TURN**	18 She's (watch) 5 videos today.	17 She's (watch) TV since 6 o'clock.	16 I've (try) to call her once already.	15 I've (try) to call her all morning.
10 I've (write) a few letters today.	11 I've (write) for an hour and my hand aches.	12 I've (walk) 10 kilometres today.	13 I've (walk) all day and I'm tired.	14 He's (play) football and his boots are muddy.
9 I've never (eat) Russian food before. **MISS YOUR TURN**	8 Have you ever (meet) a famous person?	7 We've (play) basketball and now we're tired.	6 I've (go) to Paris 3 times.	5 How long have you (wait)?
START	1 I've (learn) English for 3 years now.	2 Have you (finish) all the questions yet?	3 He's (eat) all day and now he isn't hungry.	4 They've (sit) there all day watching TV. **MISS YOUR TURN**

From **Singing Grammar** by Mark Hancock © Cambridge University Press 1998 **PHOTOCOPIABLE**

Heads (present perfect continuous): 1, 3, 4, 5, 7, 11, 13, 14, 15, 17, 21, 23
Tails (present perfect simple): 2, 6, 8, 9, 10, 12, 16, 18, 19, 20, 22

85

Songbook

Finger positions

	Chords for guitar
C dó	C, C7 (III), Cm7 (III), C7(9), C7m (III), C° C7/D (III), C#7 (IV), C#m7 (IV), C#m (IV), C#m7(9), C#m7(9) (III) C#m7/B (IV)
D ré	D, D7, Dm, Dm7, D7M, D7(#9) (V) D7(b9) (IV)
E mi	E, E7, Em, E7M, E7(9), Em7 E7(#9), Em6/G (II), E7(13), Em7(9) (VII)
F fá	F, F#, F#m, F#7, F#m7, F#7(b13) F#m7(11), F#m7(#9) (III)

Songbook: finger positions

Chords for guitar

G sol

G, G7, G7M, G6, G#, G#m7

G#7(b 13), G#m7/D#

A lá

A, A7, Am, Am7, A7(13), A6

A/G#

B si

B, B7, Bm, Bm7, B7(b9), B7(13)

B7(b13), Bm(7M), B7/4(9), Bb

KEY

bar chord, fret number, open strings

87

Songbook: lyrics and chords

Lyrics and chords

1 Johnny's playing football

```
E            A         B    E
Johnny's playing football
             A         B    E
Johnny's playing football
                A              B     E    A   B   E
He's wearing all his school clothes and getting very dirty
C#m
Johnny!
F#
Your mother's coming!
C#m
Johnny!
F#
Your mother's coming!

E            A         B    E
Mary's eating chocolate
             A         B    E
Mary's eating chocolate
                A           B       E    A   B   E
She's eating lots of chocolate and now she isn't hungry
C#m
Mary!
F#
Your dinner's ready!
C#m
Mary!
F#
Your dinner's ready!

E                A    B    E
The kids are drawing pictures
                 A    B    E
The kids are drawing pictures
                A           B     E    A   B   E
They aren't doing the exercise, they're just drawing pictures
C#m
Kids!
F#
The teacher's looking!
C#m
Kids!
F#
The teacher's looking!
```

2 Who, where, when?

This song has no chords.

Songbook: lyrics and chords

3 Getting up

```
A            D
Do you like getting up
E            D
And going to school?
No no!
A D E      D
I enjoy having fun
A            D
Do you like sitting down
E          D
And doing exams?
No no!
A D E        D
I enjoy watching films
A            D
Do you like washing up
E          D
And cleaning your room?
No no!
A D E        D
I enjoy playing games

G
I don't like housework
E
And I hate homework
G                    Bb    E7(13)
I love relaxing with my friends

A            D
Does he like getting up …
```

4 I can't hear you

```
Em7(9)
I can't hear you
A7(13)
I can't hear you sing
Em7(9)
I can't hear you
A7(13)
I can't hear you sing
D7M
Can you sing louder
    Fm7          B7(b13)
So I can hear your voice again?
D7M
Can you sing louder
    Fm7          B7(b13)
So I can hear your voice again?

Em7      A7              D7M B7(b13)
  Can you raise your hands?  (Yes I can)
Em7      A7              D7M B7(b13)
  Can you drink the sea?    (No I can't)
Em7      A7              D7M B7(b13)
  Can you clap your hands?  (Yes I can)
Em7      A7              D7M    B7(b13)
  Can you count to three?   (One, two three!)

Em7 (9)
I can't hear you …

Em7      A7              D7M B7(b13)
  Can you touch your nose?  (Yes I can)
Em7      A7              D7M B7(b13)
  Can you touch the sky?    (No I can't)
Em7      A7              D7M B7(b13)
  Can you move your toes?   (Yes I can)
Em7      A7              D7M           B7(b13)
  Can you count to five?    (One, two, three, four, five!)

Em7 (9)
I can't hear you …

Em7
Can you touch …
```

89

Songbook: lyrics and chords

5 I've got exams

```
Dm              G
  I've got exams in the afternoon
Dm              G
  I've got a lot of homework too
Dm              G
  I've got a feeling I've got flu
   F    A   Dm   G
  Why can't I be like you?

Dm              G
  You've got a tree there in the zoo
Dm              G
  You haven't got any work to do
Dm                  G
  You've got a bunch of bananas too
   F    A   Dm      D
  Why can't I be like you?

G         A
  You're just an orang-utan
D7M         Bm
  Sitting in your tree all day
G              A
  Have you got any space for me
D7M          Bm   G   A   Dm    G
  Up there in your tree toda...............y?

Dm              G
  You've got a lot of friends up there
Dm              G
  You sit around and you comb your hair
Dm                  G
  You haven't got any worries and cares
   F    A   Dm      D
  Why can't I be like you?

G
  You're just …

G
  You're just …
```

6 What a crazy day!

```
F#7
I woke up this morning

And I got into bed

Then I ate a cup of tea

And drank a slice of bread
B7       F#7      B7       F#7       C#7
Oh, what a crazy day! Oh, what a crazy day!

F#
I went to the bus stop

And caught the train to school

Then I rode my bicycle

In the swimming pool
B7       F#7      B7       F#7       C#7
Oh, what a crazy day! Oh, what a crazy day!

F#7
Someone broke the telephone

So then I rang my friend

We went to the football field

And swam from end to end
B7       F#7      B7       F#7       C#7
Oh, what a crazy day! Oh, what a crazy day!

F#7
I came home this evening

And watched the radio

I lay down on the ceiling

And read a video
B7       F#7      B7       F#7       C#7
Oh, what a crazy day! Oh, what a crazy day!
```

7 Space invader

Em   G
I'm your space invader
    F#m   B7
And I live behind your screen
Em   G
I'm your favourite alien
   F#   F   Em   G   F#m   B7
Come and play with me

Em   G
I wake up in the morning
F#m   B7
And I lie in bed and think
Em   G
I comb my hair and brush my teeth
   F#   F   Em   G   F#m   B7
And then I have a drink

A   A/G#
I know you like computer games
   F#
You know I like them too
B   A
I live in a computer
         G   F#
And there's nothing else to do

Em   G
I eat fast food for breakfast
   F#m   B7
And I read a magazine
Em   G
You switch on your computer
     F#   F   Em   G   F#m   B7
And I jump behind your screen

Em   G
I stand there with my monster friends
   F#m   B7
We wave our arms and legs
Em   G
We move around, you shoot us down
   F#   F   Em   G   F#m   B7
And then we go to bed

A
I know you like …

Em
I stand there …

8 Dream of a pizza

      E   G#   A   B
You wake up in the night
             E   G#   A   B
And you're lying on your back
      E   G#   A   B
You feel a little hungry
     E   G#   A   B
It's time for a snack

    A
You go down to the kitchen
 B
And you switch on the light
  A
You open the fridge
B   E   G#   A   B
And this is what you find
          E   G#   A   B
This is what you find …

     E   G#   A   B
You find a little cheese
       E   G#   A   B
But it isn't very nice
          E   G#   A   B
There are a few frozen peas
        E   G#   A   B
There's a lot of cooked rice

    A
You try to make a sandwich
     B
But there isn't much bread
   A
There isn't any butter
     B   E   G#   A   B
So you just go back to bed
                E   G#   A   B
You just go back to bed

        E   G#   A   B
Well, you're dreaming of a pizza
          E   G#   A   B
But there aren't any tomatoes
        E   G#   A   B
And there isn't any tuna
         E   G#   A   B
There are just a few potatoes

  A
You try …

And dream of a pizza
You dream of a pizza

Songbook: lyrics and chords

9 Blue train

```
         G7
I'm sitting on a blue train
C7
An old blue train
     G7
An old blue express train
              C7
Going down a steel track

A long steel track
     G7
A long steel railway track
            D7#9
Passing through green hills
C7
Big green hills
G7
Beautiful big green hills
Am     D7      G7
On my way back home
F          G
Home sweet home

         G7
I'm sitting on a white plane
C7
A fast white plane
     G7
A fast white passenger plane
              C7
Flying through the blue sky

The wide blue sky
     G7
The beautiful wide blue sky
            D7#9
High above the deep sea
C7
The deep green sea
G7
The wonderful deep green sea
Am    D7      G7
On my way back home
F          G
Home sweet home

Bm           Em
I'm on my way back home
A           D7
I've been away too long

         G7
I'm sitting on a blue train
C7
An old blue train
     G7
An old blue express train
```

10 Happier than the birds

```
C
  You want the same girl as me
Am
  You think you're better than me
F
  But it's easy to see
G
  She loves me

C
  You've got more money than me
Am
  You're better looking than me
F
  But it's easy to see
G
  She loves me

Am
I love her and she loves me
       G
I'm happier than the birds in the trees
Am
You've got money but can't you see
D7           G
You can't take her love from me

C
  Your work is better than mine
Am
  Your marks are higher than mine
F
  But it's easy to see
G
  She loves me

C
  You're more attractive than me
Am
  But not as happy as me
F
  Because it's easy to see
G
  She loves me

Am
I love her …
```

11 I'd like to

```
D       Em A7  D
I'd like to see you again
         Em   A   D
I'd like to be in love again

G7M       C7(9)
Would you like to
     F#m7      B7(b9)
Go out with me tonight?
Em          A7
Won't you please
Am7          D7(b9)
Give me one more chance?

G7M       C7(9)
I'd like to tell you
  F#m7     B7(B9)
I still love you
       Em           A7        D
Please say that you still love me too

D
I'd like to …
```

12 I was walking

```
                        Am7         D7
I was walking down the street one day
           G7M    G6
When I saw you
                        Am7         D7
Yeah you really took my breath away
           G7M    G6
Nothing I could do

              C7M
I was feeling down
        Cm        Bm7
You made me feel OK
          E7(b13)     Am7
And I remember to this day
                         D7
The way you looked at me

The way you made me feel

                       Am7         D7
When I saw you on the street that day
              G7M    G6
My heart went wild
                        Am7         D7
I was trying to find the words to say
              G7M    G6
When you turned and smiled

              C7M
We were standing there
          Cm        Bm7
When it began to rain
          E7(b13)    Am7
So we went to a cafe
                         D7
We walked into that room

And stayed all afternoon
```

Songbook: lyrics and chords

13 If you're lonely

```
A        B7       C#m7
  If you're tired and lonely
A    B7      C#m7
  I'll come to you
A       B7       C#m7    C#m7/B   A    A/G#     F#m
  If you need someone you can talk to
       G#7(b13)         C#7m(9)
  I'll be there for you


A       B7       C#m7
  If your friends desert you
A     B7      C#m7
  I'll be by your side
A       B7       C#m7   C#m7/B   A    A/G#    F#m
  If you need a place    to      go
        G#7(b13)       C#7m(9)
  My door is open wide


A        B7       C#m7
  If you're feeling cold
A    B7      C#m7
  I'll build a fire
A       B7       C#m7    C#m7/B   A    A/G#    F#m
  If you're feeling sad    and       low
       G#7(b13)         C#7m(9)
  I'll take you higher
```

14 Dangerous romance

```
      Am7    E7(#9)    Am7
  She came in through the door
E7(#9)    Am7    E7(#9)  Am7  E7(#9)
  Everybody looked
      Am7    E7(#9)    Am7
  He went across the floor
E7(#9)  Am7     E7(#9)   Am7   E7(#9)
  And    stood with her and talked
       Dm7
  He asked her for a dance
                        Am7    E7(#9)   Am7   E7(#9)
  They danced through the night
Dm7
  Everybody thought
               E7(#9)
  'That dance will be the last dance of their lives'

       Am7  E7(#9)  Am7
  It was a dangerous    romance
     E7(#9)      Am7    E7(#9)    Am7   E7(#9)
  But they didn't care
         Dm7
  From the first time that they danced
       E7(#9)
  It was a life or death affair

Am7      E7(#9)  Am7
  Then they left the bar
E7(#9)    Am7     E7(#9)    Am7    E7(#9)
  Everybody saw
       Am7    E7(#9) Am7
  They jumped into a   car,
E7(#9) Am7    E7(#9)     Am7     E7(#9)
  And    as they closed the door
         Dm7
  They heard somebody say
         Am7    E7(#9)   Am7  E7(#9)
  'They'll catch you both one day'
         Dm7
  But they drove onto the highway,
     E7(#9)
  And tried to get away

        Am7
  It was a dangerous ...
```

Songbook: lyrics and chords

15 Josephine

```
    E7M        G#m7/D#   C#m7
I know you've never      seen my face
         A6            B7(13)
You've never heard my name
    E7M        G#m7/C#   C#m7
Although I've never      talked to you
       A6            B7(13)    C°
I've got you on the brain

C#m7(9)      F#m7(11)   B74(9)          E7M
Jo..........sephine, I've seen you in my dreams
C#m7(9)      F#M7(11)  B74(9)   (stop)      E7M
Jo..........sephine,       I've seen you in my dreams

    E7M  G#m7/C#  C#m7
I've never had the   confidence
    A6         B7(b13)
To talk to you before
    E7M        G#m7/C#  C#m7
The time has come and here I am
    A6           B7(13)   C°
Knocking on your door

C#m7(9)
Josephine ...

    G#m7         C#7
I talked to Josephine last night
     A            B
And now she knows my name
    G#m7      C#7
I told her how I feel and then
   A6            B7(13)   C°   C#m7(9)
She looked at me as if I was   insane

F#m7(11)   B74(9)   E7M

C#m7(9)
Josephine
                  C#m7(9)   F#m7(11)
You know I've never felt so stupid before
B74(9)            E7M
Standing at Josephine's door

C#m7(9)
Josephine ...
```

16 Sweet things

```
D                C7/D
I................used to love a boy
D                C7/D            Bm       Bm(7M)
And I............used to think he loved me
      Bm7      E7(9)  A          A7
Now I know that I was wrong

D                C7/D
He...............left me for a girl
D                C7/D            Bm       Bm(7M)
Who..............used to be my friend
      Bm7            E7(9)  A
Now I know he loved her all     along

                      A/G#                  Em6/G
But he................used to say sweet things to me
      F#7(b13)       Bm7
And I always used to believe him
     E7                         A
He used to say sweet things to me
(repeat)

D                C7/D            D
He...............used me to be near her
      C7/D           Bm    Bm(7M)
Pretending that he loved me
      Bm7            E7(9)    A
All the things he used to say were lies

D                C7/D            D
Then.............one day I watched them
C7/D             Bm          Bm(7M)
Dancing in each other's arms
     Bm7    E7(9)         A       A7
That was when I re...............alized

But he ...
```

95

Songbook: lyrics and chords

17 In trouble again

```
        A7              D              A7
I was sitting in the bedroom playing my guitar one evening
                                  G            E
Then I remembered I'd started making to..........ast
        A7                    D
So I rushed downstairs and I ran into the kitchen
          A7              E          A7
But the toast had burnt and the house was full of smoke

Bm7         E     A7         D
My mother said, 'Son, look what you've done!'
       Bm7        E         A7
I said 'Oh.......... no, I'm in trouble again'

               D            A7
Saturday night I decided to invite some friends round
                                G       E
My parents had gone out, I was home alo..........ne
         A7                         D
We put the music on loud and we used the house like a playground
         A7              E            A7
We'd made an awful mess   when my friends went home

Bm7
My mother said …

A7              D             A7
Sitting on the bus, I noticed I'd forgotten my schoolbag
                                    G       E
So I went back home and found I'd forgotten my ke..........y
       A7                       D
My mother was out so I climbed in through the window
         A7        E          A7
But I slipped and fell on top of the new TV

Bm7
My mother said …
```

18 I've been waiting

```
A
I've been waiting for an hour and she's not here yet
                   E
Maybe she's stood me up
A                              D
It's been raining all the time and my hair is wet
A    E     A
Now I feel fed up

         D                       A
I've been seeing her for over two weeks now
E                            A
  I thought she was mine, all mine
              D                    A
We've been going out dancing almost every night
E                        A
  I thought everything was fine

I've been waiting for two hours, standing here alone
                                 E
I've been trying to call her on the phone
         A
I've been cursing, I've been screaming
                  D
'Cause for two weeks I've been dreaming
           A      E      A
Now the only thing to do is go back home

         D
I've been seeing her …
```